SketchUp Pro 2013
step by step

By João Gaspar

1st Edition
GetPro Books

São Paulo
2013

SketchUp Pro 2013 step by step
Gaspar, João
ISBN 978-85-61453-18-3

SketchUp Pro 2013
step by step

By João Gaspar

http://www.thesketchupbook.com
Phone (+ 55 11) 3814 8145

To Mr. Gaspar, Ms. Maria, Malu, Gabriel, Marina and all my family
To Alexandre and all those who are a part of or have been a part of GetPro Books
To all my friends

SketchUp Pro 2013 step by step

text and coordination
João Gaspar

cover
Alexandre Villares and Leonardo Reitano

final revision
João Gaspar and Alexandre Villares

translation
Kevin Thompson

layout
Camila Ghendov

contribution
Willian Belo

Julio Britto

Artur Cordeiro

Bruno Cunha

Camila Ghendov

João Carlos Kuhn

Natália Lorenzo

Caio Mamede

Ari Miaciro

Vitor Nagoya

Tobias de São Pedro

Diego Quattrone

Carolina Scatolini

Fernando Setoguchi

Mariana Suzuki

Lia Takata

Fábio Tutibachi

epub version
Leonardo Reitano

Introduction

Created to provide an experience closer to drawing and modeling with real objects, SketchUp has won over a host of loyal users year after year.

SketchUp stands out for its speed and ease when creating volumetric objects and studies.

The unique presentation quality that strays from the standards normally used and the ability to exchange information between various programs in the CAD industry are also important distinctions.

The program also brings other innovations such as integration with Google Earth and the availability of various free libraries, through the 3D Warehouse.

The book, **SketchUp Pro 2013 step by step**, aims to provide a high quality learning experience. All the described procedures are illustrated; at the end of each chapter is a summary of the main topics addressed and exercises to be downloaded at http://www.thesketchupbook.com. The site also has a discussion forum for the book and program with participation of the Author.

How to use this book

The chapters of this book were structured to provide a high quality learning experience. We believe you will be able to quickly find all the information that you need in both the first reading and those thereafter. To facilitate an understanding of the book's structure, review the following descriptions.

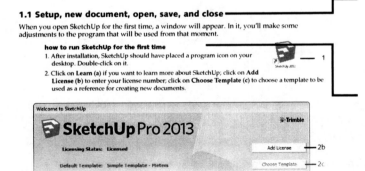

Beginning of a chapter

The title of a chapter is always part of a work objective, or a question about the program that serves as a hook for the explanations of the chapter.

This text answers the question in the title and gives general ideas about what will be explained ahead.

This is the list of topics to be covered in the chapter. These topics will always be in the upper part of the page to make them easier to locate.

Topics and procedures

This is the title of the topic. Right after will always be a small text that shows what will be discussed ahead.

Each topic consists of a series of procedures. Each procedure always indicates how to complete an operation and is almost always accompanied by screenshots from the program in use.

When necessary, some procedures are followed by notes and other important tips.

Chapter highlights

Units, location, template (p. 23)
In the **Model Info** menu, choose the units, project location and the template file. To do this, choose **Model Info/Units**, **Model Info/Location**, and **Preferences/Template** menus.

Basic viewing (p. 29)
To zoom in or out with the mouse, roll the click wheel. To **orbit**, click and drag the click wheel; to view as a **Panoramic** (*Pan*), click and drag the click wheel, and without releasing it, click and drag with the left button.

Types of selection (p. 32)
To select a line, use the **Select** tool, and click once on the desired line. To select a face, use the **Select** tool and click on the desired face. To select an object, choose Select tool, triple-click on any part of the object and SketchUp will select all the lines and faces. Same tool.

Basic drawing (p. 33)
Line: Click and drag the cursor in the direction the line will be created. Release it where you want to stop.
Irregular polygon: Click and release the cursor in the direction the line will be created. Click to confirm the end of the first line, click for each segment and click on the original point to finish.
Rectangle: Click and release the cursor in one...

Suggested activities

Ex. 01 – Setup
1. Open a new document or the **Cap01_Ex01.skp** file.
2. Configure the file to use meters or inches, in your city (for New York, use the coordinates 73°W, 40°N, and -4h00 GMT time zone).
3. Save the file in the **My Documents** folder, for Windows, or **Document**, on a Mac. Use the name **SketchUp Template**.
4. Use this file as a template for creating new documents.

Ex. 02 – Basic Drawing and Push/Pull
1. Open the **Cap01_Ex02.skp** file and draw the image below (*figs. 01a* and *01b*) with the exact measurements.

Chapter highlights

At the end of each chapter is a summary of what was covered, with small texts referring to the main explanation, for quick consultation.

Suggested activities

Lastly, there are some suggested activities related to the content of the chapter, enabling you to practice and perfect the suggested techniques. Some activities require exercises that can be downloaded from the website (see the topic **How to use the material available on the site**).

Important

This book was written from the 2013 version of SketchUp Pro for PC. On the Macintosh platform, some tools and menus may be presented somewhat differently, and these differences are mentioned in this book.

How to use the material available on the site

GetPro Books (www.getprobooks.com) created a site exclusively for this book with a forum for communication between readers, in addition to files that should be downloaded to supplement the suggested activities at the end of each chapter. To take advantage of the material available on the site:

1. Go to http://www.thesketchupbook.com.

2. Complete the form with your name and email.

3. After registration, click this link to download the **suggested activities**.

4. Click this link to access the discussion forum.

5. The suggested exercises for each chapter are available in .zip format. A .zip file exists for each chapter of the book, and you can download them by clicking directly on each link.

6. It's recommended, but not mandatory, that you create a folder for storing all your files. Don't forget to decompress the .zip files using WinZip or a Windows extraction tool before beginning work. If using a Mac, use a program like Stuffit Expander to extract the exercises.

If an instruction above contradicts what is published on our site at the time the book is purchased, please contact us by email at support@thesketchupbook.com, so we can inform you on how to access the material on the site.

Where to get help

Below is a list with some recommended sites and other publications that can help to improve your knowledge of the program:

1. For more information on using SketchUp, visit http://sketchup.google.com/support.

2. To download ready-made-use objects on SketchUp, visit http://sketchup.google.com/3dwarehouse.

3. To see video tutorials, in addition to work done using SketchUp, access http://www.youtube.com and type SketchUp in the search box.

Table of contents

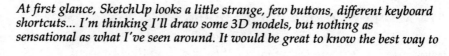

At first glance, SketchUp looks a little strange, few buttons, different keyboard shortcuts... I'm thinking I'll draw some 3D models, but nothing as sensational as what I've seen around. It would be great to know the best way to

start using SketchUp!

SketchUp was created for those wanting to produce 3D objects in a fast, easy, and intuitive way. The program comes with a totally unusual interface, in which the creation, manipulation, and editing of elements is done in a way that is different from any other software. Given its unique characteristics, it doesn't fall into the category of CAD software (like Vectorworks, ArchiCAD, or Revit, for example), or in that of traditional 3D software (3D Studio, Maya, Cinema 4D, and others); and that is what makes it such a special program.

What you'll read in this chapter

1.1 Setup, new document, open, save, and close

1.2 Dealing with toolbars – Windows version

1.3 Dealing with toolbars – Mac version

1.4 Units, location, template

1.5 Basic viewing

1.6 Types of selection

1.7 Basic drawing

1.8 Draw with measurements

1.9 How to create and alter basic volumes

1.10 How to delete objects

1.1 Setup, new document, open, save, and close

When you open SketchUp for the first time, a window will appear. In it, you'll make some adjustments to the program that will be used from that moment.

how to run SketchUp for the first time

1. After installation, SketchUp should have placed a program icon on your desktop. Double-click on it.

2. Click on **Learn** (a) if you want to learn more about SketchUp; click on **Add License** (b) to enter your license number; click on **Choose Template** (c) to choose a template to be used as a reference for creating new documents.

3. After clicking **Choose Template** (item **2c**) click again to choose one of the options (use the click wheel to see all):

   a. **Simple Template – Feet and Inches**: Displays the basic settings for styles and colors, with units in feet and inches;
   b. **Simple Template – Meters**: Displays the basic settings of styles and colors, with units in meters;
   c. **Architectural Design – Feet and inches**: Configured for architecture, in feet and inches;
   d. **Architectural Design – Millimeters**: Configured for architecture, in millimeters;
   e. **Google Earth Modeling – Feet and Inches**: Adjusted for use with Google Earth, in feet and inches;
   f. **Google Earth Modeling – Meters**: Adjusted for use with Google Earth, in meters;
   g. **Engineering – Feet**: Configured for engineering, units in feet;
   h. **Engineering – Meters**: Configured for engineering, units in meters;
   i. **Product Design and Woodworking – Inches**: Adjusted for woodworking and product design, in inches;
   j. **Product Design and Woodworking – Millimeters**: Adjusted for woodworking and product design, in millimeters;
   k. **Plan View – Feet and Inches**: Simple configuration for plan view, in feet and inches;
   l. **Plan View – Meters**: Simple configuration for plan view, in meters.
   m. **Beginning Template – Feet and Inches**: Template to be used with official SketchUp training material, in feet and inches;
   n. **Beginning Template – Meters**: Template to be used with official SketchUp training material, in meters.

4. Click on **Start using SketchUp** and the program will start, using the selection made on the previous item.

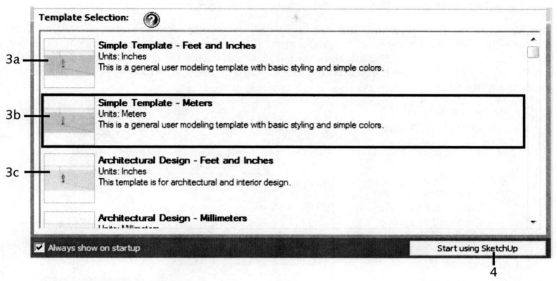

to create a new document

1. Choose **File/New** (*Ctrl+N*).

2. SketchUp will open a new drawing area. Your configurations (units, location, palette, etc.) are based on the selected **template** file, which can be found in **Window/Preferences/Template**.

to open a document

1. Choose **File/Open** (*Ctrl+O*), and select the document to be opened.

> **NOTE** SketchUp for Windows does not allow opening more than one document during the same session of the program. If you want to open two or more documents (to copy and paste objects between them, for example) you need to open other sessions of SketchUp, clicking twice on the program icon (just as if starting the program again). On a Macintosh, SketchUp allows using more than one document during the same session. To toggle between files on a Mac, just use the **Window** menu.

to save a document

1. Choose **File/Save** (*Ctrl+S*).

2. If it is the first time the document will be saved, SketchUp will ask for a name and location on the computer.

3. If it's not the first time, the document will be saved under the same name with which it was created and in the same place.

4. To save a document with another name and/or place it in another location on the computer, choose **File/Save As....**

to close a document and end the program

1. Choose **File/Exit** (*Ctrl+Q*). If the document has not been saved, SketchUp will ask if you want to save it. The program will never close your document without saving (unless that is your intention).

1.2 Dealing with Toolbars – Windows version

SketchUp does have a lot of tools that are organized in toolbars. As the software became more flexible along the years because of the popularity of the add-ons (extra tools you can download to increase SketchUp skills), the interface usually can get a little bit clunky, with a lot of toolbars floating on your screen. Next, you'll learn how to manage SketchUp toolbars to keep your drawing window organized.

to open a toolbar

1. Choose **View/Toolbars....**

2. Activate the toolbar you want by clicking in the related check box. The toolbar will be shown instantly. Click once again in the box to deactivate it.

3. Once you´re done, click on **Close.**

creating a new toolbar

1. Choose **View/Toolbars.....**

2. Click on **New....**

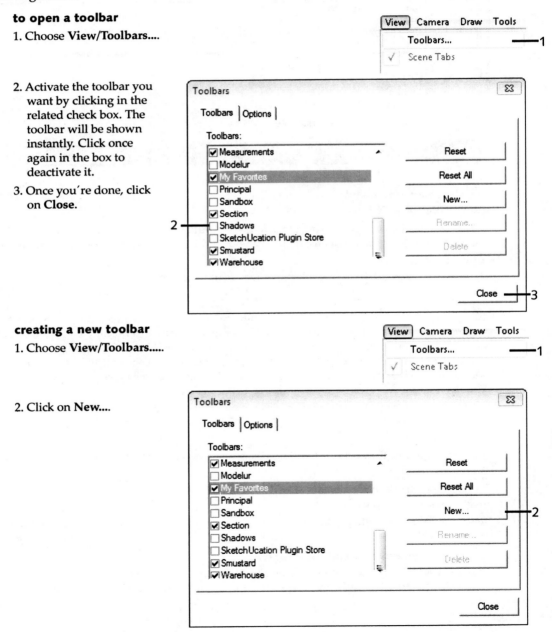

3. Enter a name for your toolbar (**a**) and click **OK** (**b**).

4. To populate your toolbar, simply click and drag the tools you want from other toolbars. Now you know you can do the same thing to reorganize existing toolbars, if you want.

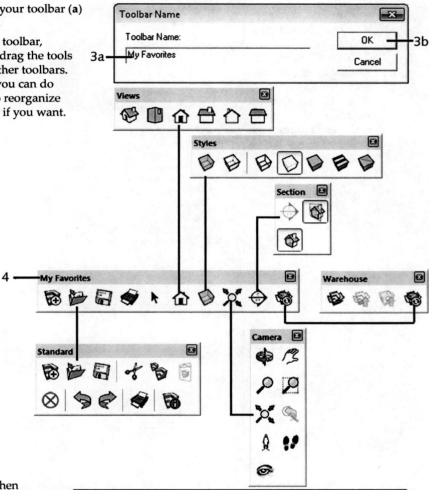

5. Click on **Close** when finished.

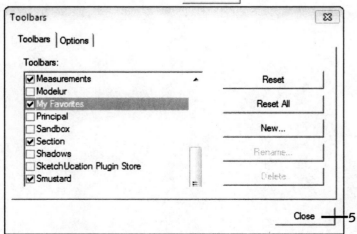

other toolbar options

1. If you have made some changes in a toolbar and now want it to be just like it was on the start, select it (**a**) and choose **Reset** (**b**). A dialog will appear asking if you really want to reset the toolbar. Choose **Yes** (**c**).

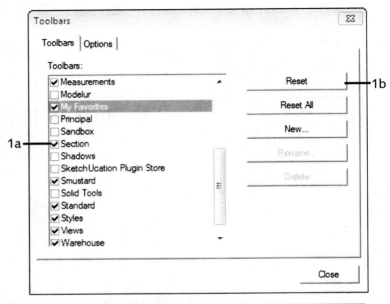

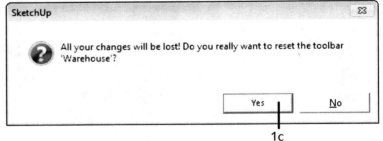

2. Click **Reset All** (**a**) to SketchUp turn all toolbars to its original state. Once again, a dialog will be shown, waiting for the confirmation of the action. Click on **Yes** (**a**).

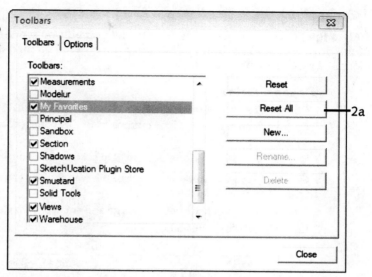

3. You can also **Rename** (**a**) or **Delete** (**b**) only the toolbars you´ve created.

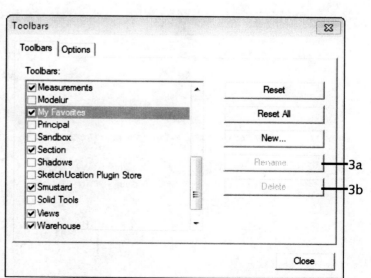

1.3 Dealing with Toolbars – Mac version

Unlike the PC version, SketchUp for Mac let you edit only one toolbar, located on the upper side of the drawing window. You can't modify the other SketchUp default toolbars, such as Solid Tools, Google, Warehouse and so on.

to open a toolbar

1. Choose **View/Customize Toolbars....**

2. Now you can drag any of the buttons from this panel (**a**) into the upper toolbar (**b**).

3. You can also drag the default SketchUp set into the toolbar.

4. Chose one of these options to change the way the buttons are displayed on SketchUp interface.

5. Click the box to change between large and small button sizes.

6. Click **Done** when finished.

Drag your favorite items into the toolbar...

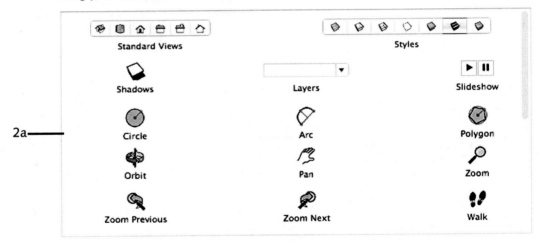

... or drag the default set into the toolbar.

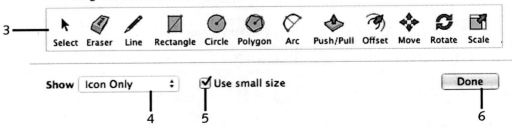

1.4 Units, location, template

The items listed above are the main configurations among various that exist in SketchUp. The idea of this topic is to show how to alter these parameters and create a new template that serves as your starting point in SketchUp.

to configure units

1. Choose **Window/ Model Info** and select the **Units** option.

2. In the **Format** field, select **Architectural** to work with feet and inches or **Decimal** if you use meters or centimenters (**a**). If you'd like, alter the **Precision** field (**b**) to 1/2" or 0,00m (two decimal places).

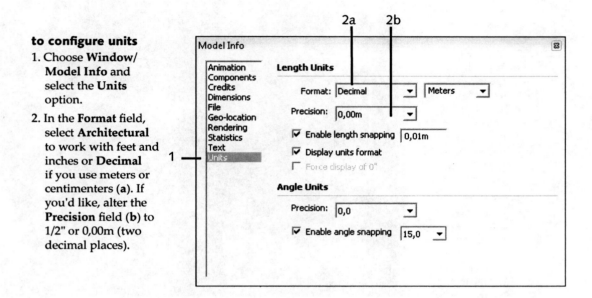

to choose a location for your project

1. Choose **Window/Model Info** and select the **Geo-location** option.

2. Click on **Add Location....**

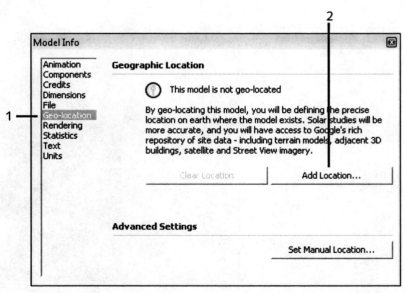

3. Click on the indicated field and type the name of your project's location (**a**). Next, click on **Search** (**b**).

4. SketchUp will display the indicated location in the window. You can use the left button on your mouse and the click wheel to adjust the position according to the exact location of your project.

5. Click on **Select Region** (**a**) to select the portion of the image that you want. Next, click and drag the indicated controls (**b**) to define the area to be used. To confirm, click on **Grab** (**c**).

6. Notice that the image was inserted into your drawing and the **Geo-Location** panel now displays the correct geographic information (including the correctly displayed solar north).

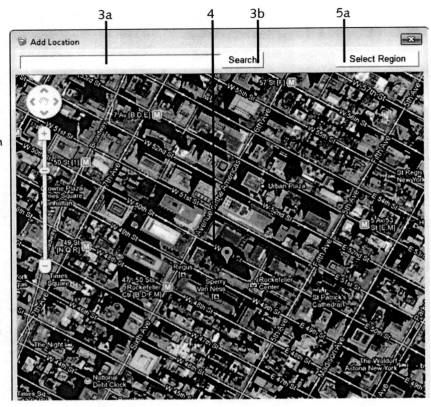

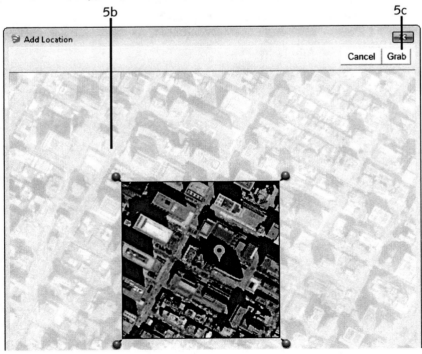

viewing option

Importing from Google Earth to SketchUp always brings two objects: one is the flat image, without topographic information, and the other is a group comprised of the topography and the applied image.

1. To alternate between the terrain image without topography and the group, with topography, choose **Google** toolbar and click on **Toggle Terrain**.

to manually configure the location of the project

1. Choose **Window/ Model Info** and select the **Geo-location** option.

2. Click on **Set Manual Location**....

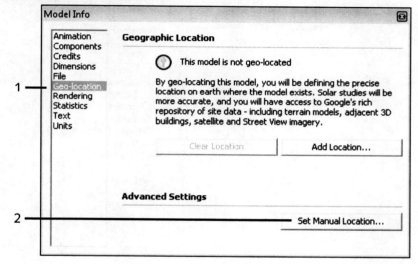

3. Adjust the items in the box:

   a. **Country**: Type the name of the country where the project is;
   b. **Location**: Write the name of the location of your project;
   c. **Latitude**: Enter the latitude of your project;
   d. **Longitude**: Enter the longitude of your project.
4. Click on **OK** to confirm.

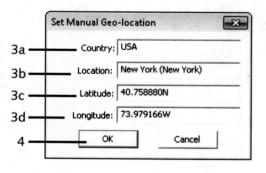

to set project north manually

The exact location you've manually set refers to the SketchUp drawing origin and the north angle is automatically aligned to the green axis. To alter the north angle you have to download the Solar North extension from the Extension Warehouse. Learn how to do that on page **199**. After downloading the add-on, you can set the north angle by doing the steps as described below.

1. Choose **View/Toolbars...** (**a**) and turn on the **Solar North** toolbar (**b**). Next, click **OK** (**c**).

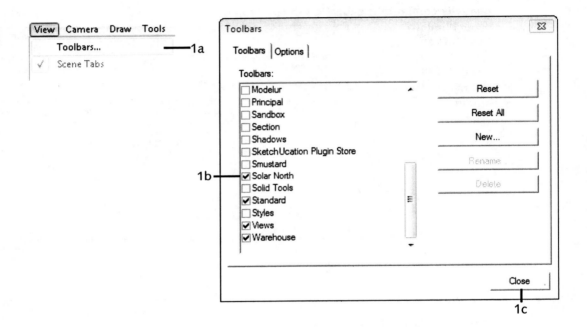

2. Click on the indicated button to activate the north indicator in the drawing area.

3. Click this button if you want to indicate north using the compass (**a**). Click on any point (**b**) and drag the mouse in the direction you want to mark north; release the button to confirm (**c**).

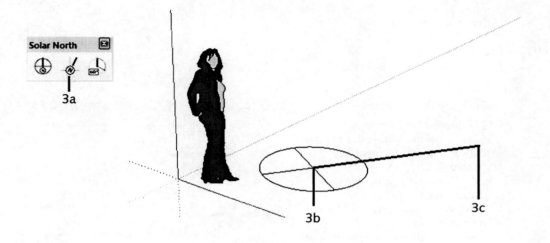

4. Click on this button to type a value for north in the box (**a**). Click **OK** to confirm (**b**).

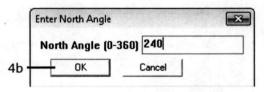

to create a template

1. Configure the file (units, location, and any other type of information, including drawings, if needed) and save it using the **File/Save As Template...** menu option.

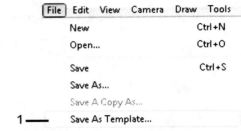

2. Configure the items in the box:

   a. **Name:** Name the template;
   b. **Description:** Write a short text that summarizes the template characteristics;
   c. **File Name:** Name the file that contains the template;
   d. **Set as default template:** Click this box if you want the template to be used automatically each time SketchUp is started.
3. Click on **Save** to save the template.

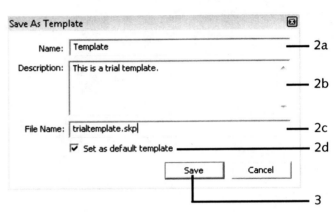

to choose a template

1. Choose **Window/Preferences**.

2. In the box that opens, choose **Template** (**a**); then select a template from the list (**b**).

3. Click on **OK**. This template will be used as a reference the next time you start SketchUp.

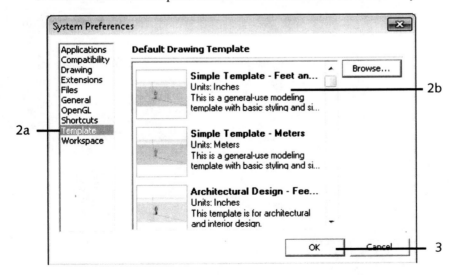

1.5 Basic viewing

You can control the most important view commands directly from the mouse. However, there are some more complex movements that can only be done using the menus and toolbars.

to zoom in and out
1. On the **Camera** toolbar, choose the **Zoom** tool.
2. Place the cursor in the center of the screen, then click and drag up (zoom in) and down (zoom out).

NOTE To zoom in or out with the mouse, roll the click wheel.

to orbit a project
1. On the **Camera** toolbar, choose the **Orbit** tool.
2. Place the cursor in the center of the screen; click and drag to orbit. If you hold **Shift** while clicking and dragging the cursor, SketchUp will move in a panoramic mode.

NOTE To orbit with the mouse, click and drag the click wheel.

to magnify a particular area
1. On the **Camera** toolbar, choose the **Zoom Window** tool.
2. Click once to indicate where the area to be magnified starts (**a**). Drag the cursor and release it where you want the zoom window to end (**b**).

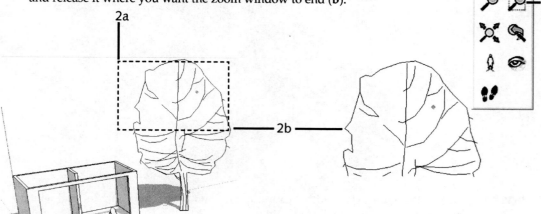

NOTE If you are too zoomed out on a project, go to the **Camera** toolbar and choose the **Zoom Extents** button for SketchUp to frame the project in the screen.

to view as a Panoramic (Pan)

1. On the **Camera** toolbar, choose the **Panoramic** (*Pan*) tool.

2. Place the cursor in the center of the screen, click and drag to either side to move the viewer.

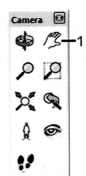

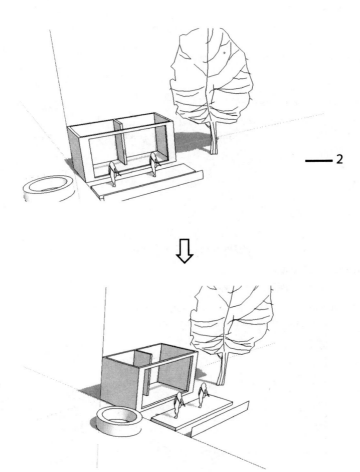

—— 2

NOTE To view as a **Panoramic** (*Pan*) with the mouse, click and drag the click wheel, and without releasing it, click and drag with the left button.

how to place the viewer inside the project

1. Choose **Camera/Standard Views/Top**.

2. On the **Camera** toolbar, choose the **Position Camera** tool.

3. Click where you want to position the viewer and hold the mouse button (**a**).
   Release the button in the direction the viewer will be looking (**b**).

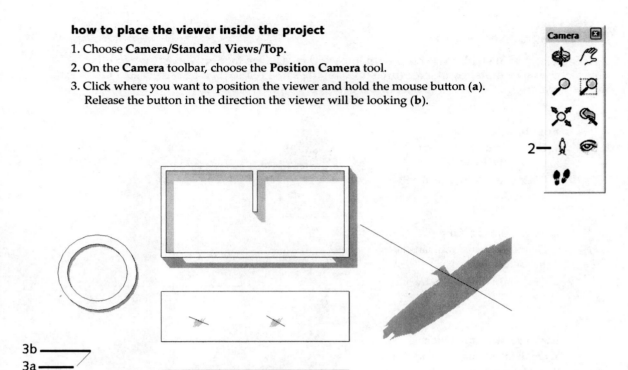

4. In the **Measurements** toolbar, type the height of the viewer; next, press **Enter.**

5. Next, SketchUp will automatically activate the **Look Around** tool. Click and drag to move the
   viewer without moving it out of place.

1.6 Types of selection

All the objects in SketchUp are built with lines and faces. One face only exists when it is completely surrounded by at least three lines on the same plane. You can select several lines and faces, therefore transforming the set into a group or component.

how to select a line

1. On the **Principal** toolbar, choose the **Select** tool.

2. Click once directly on the line you want.

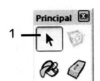

how to select a face

1. On the **Principal** toolbar, choose the **Select** tool.

2. Click once directly on the face you want.

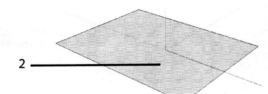

how to select an object

1. On the **Principal** toolbar, choose the **Select** tool.

2. Click three times on any element of the object to select all the lines and faces connected to it.

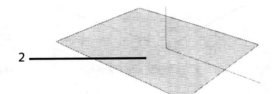

to select more than one object

1. On the **Principal** toolbar, choose the **Select** tool.

2. Triple-click on the first object to be selected.

3. Press and hold the **Shift** key, and triple-click on the other objects to select them.

4. If you click three times on an object that has already been selected, it will be released from the selection.

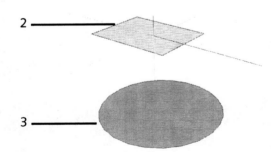

other interesting options

1. By double-clicking a line, the line and all the faces connected to it will be selected.

2. By double-clicking a face, the face and all the lines connected to it will be selected.

3. Some options for editing objects only appear when you click the right mouse button. In this case, SketchUp shows the context menu. The information on this menu (which varies according to the object selected) is mentioned, always when necessary, throughout the book.

1.7 Basic drawing

In SketchUp you draw directly in 3D, and the basic shapes (even arcs and circles) are actually built with lines. These tools are the foundation for building volumes, as we'll see later.

line

1. On the **Drawing** toolbar, choose the **Pencil** tool.

2. Click and drag the cursor in the direction the line will be created. Release it where you want to stop.

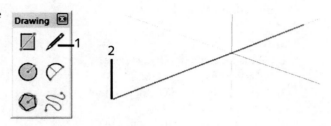

> **NOTE** If you click and release, instead of clicking and dragging, SketchUp will start another line at the end of the current line.

irregular polygon

1. On the **Drawing** toolbar, choose the **Pencil** tool.

2. Click and release the cursor in the direction the line will be created. Click to confirm the end of the first line.

3. Notice that SketchUp already begins to trace a new line. Click for each segment, and click on the original point to finish.

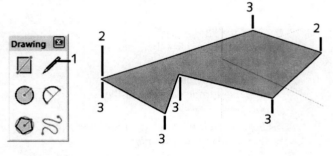

> **NOTE** To stop drawing the polygon, press **ESC**.

rectangle

1. On the **Drawing** toolbar, choose the **Rectangle** tool.

2. Click and release the cursor on the rectangle starting point.

3. Move the cursor diagonally and click where you want to place the opposite vertex.

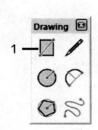
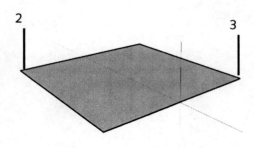

circle

1. On the **Drawing** toolbar, choose the **Circle** tool.

2. Click and release the cursor on the starting point for the circle.

3. Move the cursor to determine the radius and click to finish.

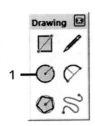 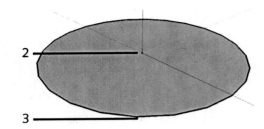

arc

1. On the **Drawing** toolbar, choose the **Arc** tool.

2. Click and release the cursor on the starting point of the arc.

3. Move the cursor to determine the end of the arc and click again.

4. Move the cursor to choose the size of the bow and click again to finish.

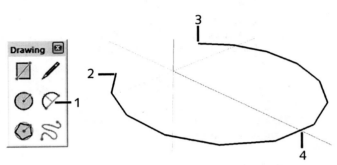

regular polygon

1. On the **Drawing** toolbar, choose the **Polygon** tool.

2. In the **Measurements** toolbar, type the number of sides of the polygon.

3. Click and release the cursor to start drawing the polygon.

4. Move the cursor and click when you reach the desired distance.

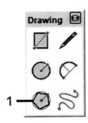 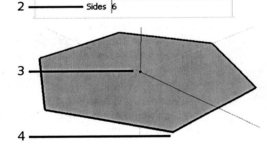

freehand

1. On the **Drawing** toolbar, choose the **Freehand** tool.

2. Click and drag the cursor to draw however you want. To stop, just release the button.

 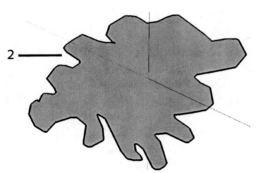

1.8 Drawing with measurements

SketchUp also allows entering exact measurements at the time an object is created. To do this, use the **Measurements** toolbar in the lower right portion of the SketchUp window.

to draw a line or polygon with measurements

1. On the **Drawing** toolbar, choose the **Pencil** tool.

2. Click where you want to start the line and move in the desired direction.

3. In the **Measurements** toolbar, type the dimension and press **Enter**. The line was drawn in the indicated direction.

4. At this point, SketchUp will start a new line at the end of the current one. Press **ESC** if you want to stop drawing.

5. Move the cursor in the direction of the next segment and type a number in the **Measurements** toolbar. Press **Enter**.

6. Repeat items **4** and **5** to create new lines. To stop, click again on the starting point (to close the polygon, creating a face) or press **ESC** (keep the polygon open).

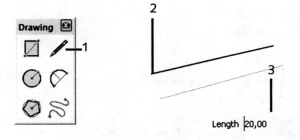

Length 20,00

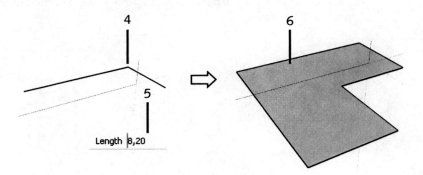

Length 8,20

how to draw a rectangle with measurements

1. On the **Drawing** toolbar, choose the **Rectangle** tool.

2. Click where you want to start the rectangle (**a**) and move the cursor in the desired direction (**b**).

3. In the **Measurements** toolbar, type the rectangle dimensions in **X,Y** (or **X;Y**, in some countries) format. Press **Enter** to complete the rectangle.

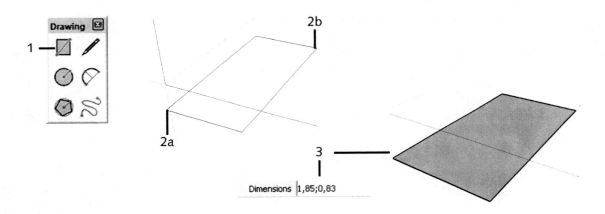

how to draw a circle or regular polygon with measurements

1. On the **Drawing** toolbar, choose the **Circle** or **Polygon** tool.

2. In the **Measurements** toolbar, type the number of lines that will complete the circle or regular polygon (note that for SketchUp the difference between them is only the number of sides). Press **Enter**.

3. Then click and release the cursor on the starting point of the circle.

4. Move the cursor to determine the radius and type the desired number in the **Measurements** toolbar. Press **Enter**.

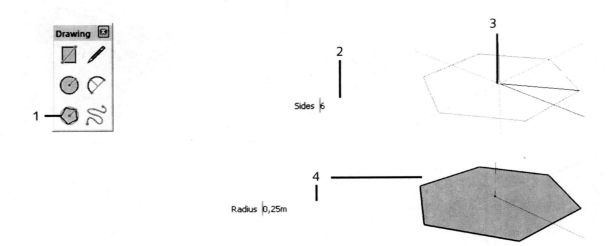

1.9 How to create and alter basic volumes

Starting from a drawing of simple elements, SketchUp is capable of creating tridimensional shapes quite easily. You can create new objects from existing figures in a way that's fast and innovative.

to create volumes from a face

1. On the **Edit** toolbar, choose the **Push/Pull** tool.

2. Move the cursor over the desired face. Notice that SketchUp highlights the selected face with a different shade.

3. Click on the face and move it in the desired direction.

4. If you want to determine a dimension, type it in the **Measurements** toolbar at this time. Press **Enter** to finish the object.

5. If you didn't enter any number (item **4**), just click when it reaches the desired size.

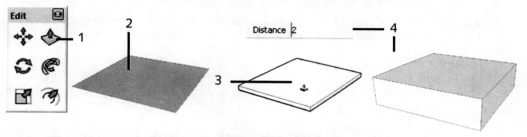

how to create new volumes from others, using Push/Pull

1. Over the face of any 3D object, draw a new one with tools from the **Drawing** toolbar.

2. On the **Edit** toolbar, choose the **Push/Pull** tool.

3. Move the cursor over the new face. Notice that SketchUp highlights the selected face with a different shade.

4. Click on the surface and move it in the desired direction (in or out of the original object). If you want to determine a dimension, type it in the **Measurements** toolbar. Press **Enter** to finish the object.

5. If you didn't enter any number (item **4**), just click when it's moved to where you wanted.

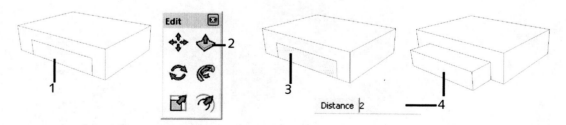

> **NOTE** If you press **Ctrl** when using **Push/Pull**, SketchUp creates a new object, but keeps the lines of the original volume.

1.10 How to delete objects

You can delete objects using the **Delete** button or the **Eraser** tool, which removes one or more lines at a time.

using the keyboard to delete lines, faces, or objects

1. Select the line(s), face(s), or object(s) you want to delete.

2. Press the **Delete** button to delete. The **Backspace** key (the large key for deleting, used in various programs) does not work in SketchUp.

how to delete using the eraser tool

1. It's not necessary to select any object.

2. Choose the **Eraser** tool.

3. Click the line you wish to delete. The face(s) connected to these line(s) will be automatically deleted.

4. If preferred, click and hold the mouse button while passing the eraser over the lines you wish to eliminate. All the faces connected to these lines will be deleted.

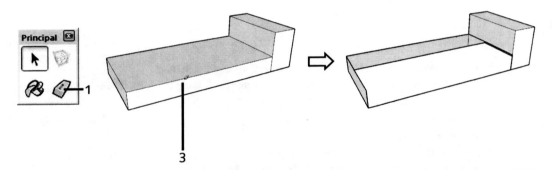

NOTE The **Eraser** doesn't delete object faces, only the lines.

Chapter highlights

Units, location, template (p. 23)

In the **Model Info** menu, choose the units, project location and the template file. To do this, choose **Model Info/Units**, **Model Info/Location**, and **Preferences/Template** menus.

Basic viewing (p. 29)

To zoom in or out with the mouse, roll the click wheel. To **orbit**, click and drag the click wheel; to view as a **Panoramic** (*Pan*), click and drag the click wheel, and without releasing it, click and drag with the left button.

Types of selection (p. 32)

To select a line, use the **Select** tool, and click once on the desired line. To select a face, use the **Select** tool and click on the desired face. To select an object, choose **Select** tool, triple-click on any part of the object and SketchUp will select all the lines and faces connected to it.

Basic drawing (p. 33)

Line: Click and drag the cursor in the direction the line will be created. Release it where you want to stop.

Irregular polygon: Click and release the cursor in the direction the line will be created. Click to confirm the end of the first line; click for each segment and click on the original point to finish.

Rectangle: Click and release the cursor on the rectangle starting point, move the cursor diagonally and click where you want to place the opposite vertex.

Circle: Click and release the cursor on the starting point for the circle; move the cursor to determine the radius and click to finish.

Arc: Click and release the cursor on the starting point of the arc; move the cursor to determine the end of the arc and click again. Move the cursor to choose the size of the bow and click again to finish.

Polygon: In the **Measurements** toolbar, type the number of sides of the polygon; click and release the cursor to start drawing the polygon. Move the cursor and click when you reach the desired distance.

Drawing with measurements (p. 35)

SketchUp also allows entering exact dimensions at the time an object is created. To do this, use the **Measurements** toolbar in the lower right portion of the SketchUp window.

Create objects with volumes using Push/Pull (p. 37)

Move the cursor over the desired face. Notice that SketchUp highlights the selected face with a different shade; click on in and move in the desired direction; click when you figure the desired size.

Suggested activities

Ex. 01 – Setup

1. Open a new document or the **Cap01_Ex01.skp** file.
2. Configure the file to use meters or inches, in your city (for New York, use the coordinates 73°W, 40°N, and -4h00 GMT time zone).
3. Save the file in the **My Documents** folder, for Windows, or **Document**, on a Mac. Use the name **SketchUp Template**.
4. Use this file as a template for creating new documents.

Ex. 02 – Basic Drawing and Push/Pull

1. Open the **Cap01_Ex02.skp** file and draw the image below (*figs. 01a* and *01b*) with the exact measurements.

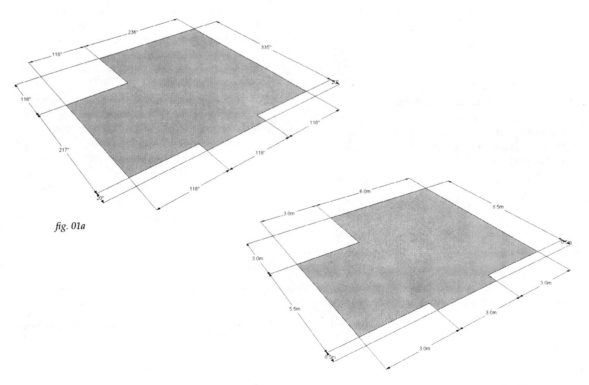

fig. 01a

fig. 01b

2. Use the **Push/Pull** tool to create a new figure with a height of 118" or 3m (*figs. 02a* and *02b*).

3. Make the following changes to the object, according to *figs. 03a* and *03b*.

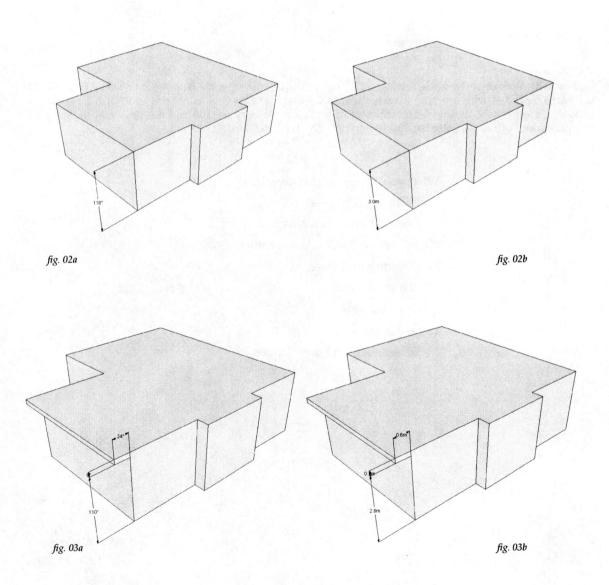

fig. 02a

fig. 02b

fig. 03a

fig. 03b

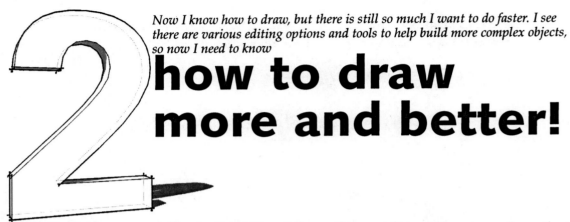

Now I know how to draw, but there is still so much I want to do faster. I see there are various editing options and tools to help build more complex objects, so now I need to know

how to draw more and better!

Just as with the basic drawing tools, SketchUp editing tools operate in a different way than other software. Some classic functions from various CAD programs like mirroring and multi matrix copying, are present in SketchUp in a subtle form. Other very useful and advanced editing options, like Follow Me, are available exclusively in SketchUp.

What you'll read in this chapter

2.1 Editing techniques

2.2 Duplication techniques

2.3 Advanced editing and creation of objects

2.4 Drawing roof faces

2.5 Placing 3D texts

2.6 Drawing aids

2.7 Sectioning objects

2.8 Dimensions and annotations

2.1 Editing techniques

The primary editing tools for objects on SketchUp are similar to those of other programs. However, depending on the manner in which they are used, they can bring surprising results.

to rotate an object

1. Select the object (a line, face, or figure).

2. On the **Edit** toolbar, choose the **Rotate** tool.

3. Click on the point that will serve as the axis of rotation (the center of the axis doesn't need to be on the selected object).

4. Move the cursor to indicate the direction of the axis of rotation and click again.

5. If you want to rotate an object with a fixed angle, type it in the **Measurements** toolbar and press **Enter**.

6. If you didn't enter a value, click when the object is in the desired position.

> **NOTE** When you select a line or face on an object and execute the rotation command, SketchUp rotates the object and to keep it connected to others, creates new faces and lines in an effect called **Autofold**.

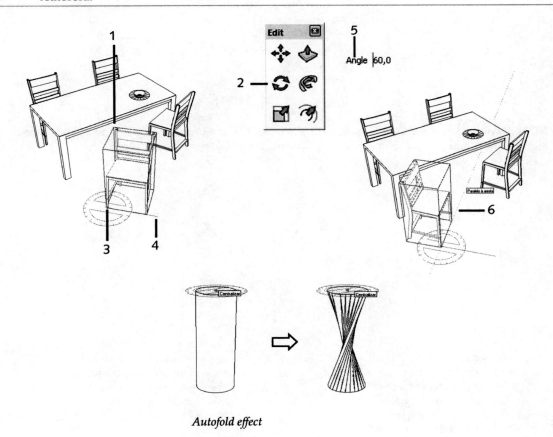

Autofold effect

how to move an object

1. Select the object (a line, face, or figure).

2. On the **Edit** toolbar, choose the **Move** tool.

3. Click on any point of the drawing and move it (the point to be moved doesn't need to be on the selected object).

4. Move the cursor to indicate the direction of movement.

5. If you'd like, type a number in the **Measurements** toolbar and press **Enter**, completing the move.

6. If you didn't type a number, click when you want to stop moving.

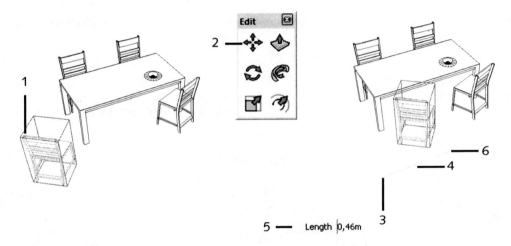

NOTE If you select lines and/or faces of an object, press **Alt**, and use the **Move** tool, SketchUp creates new lines and/or faces in any direction. SketchUp calls this resource **Autofold**.

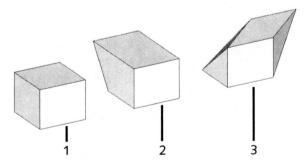

Image **1**, shows a cube without changes. The effect of normal movement of a line in a cube is shown in image **2**. The line moves on the same plane in which it was created.

Image **3** shows that by pressing **Alt** we can use the **Autofold** effect, which permits moving a line beyond the plane on which it was originally created.

to scale an object

1. Select an object.

2. On the **Edit** toolbar, choose the **Scale** tool.

3. Various control points will appear. Each one scales the object in a different way. Click on one of the control points and move the cursor.

4. If you'd like, type a scale factor in the **Measurements** toolbar and press **Enter** to execute the scale command.

5. If you didn't type any value, click when you want to execute the command.

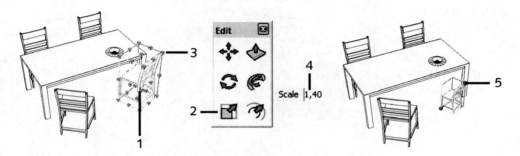

> **NOTE** When you execute the **Scale** command, SketchUp may create new faces and lines with **Autofold**, when necessary.

how to mirror an object

1. Select an object.

2. On the **Edit** toolbar, choose the **Scale** tool.

3. Various control points will appear. Click on one of the **central** control points and move the cursor.

4. Type **-1** in the **Measurements** toolbar and press **Enter** to mirror.

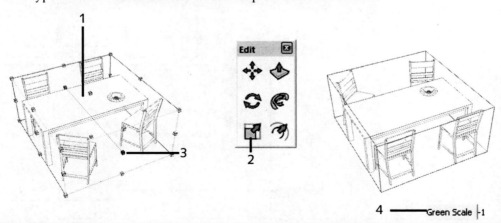

> **NOTE** It's not possible to execute a mirror operation and keep a copy of the object in the original location. It's not possible to use an external reference line to an object for mirroring, as in other design programs.

to scale an entire project

This procedure is very useful when a project has been done without measurements because it scales all elements of the drawing to the correct size.

1. On the **Construction** toolbar, choose the **Tape Measure** tool.

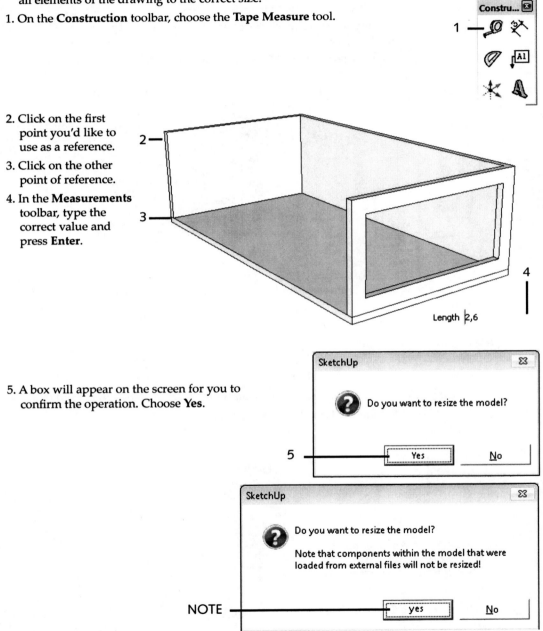

2. Click on the first point you'd like to use as a reference.

3. Click on the other point of reference.

4. In the **Measurements** toolbar, type the correct value and press **Enter**.

5. A box will appear on the screen for you to confirm the operation. Choose **Yes**.

> **NOTE** If your project contains components imported from the **Components** window, a box will open, advising you that they won't be scaled. In this case, click **Yes** to continue to scale the model.

to create new edges with the Offset tool

1. On the **Edit** toolbar, choose the **Offset** tool.
2. Move the cursor over the desired face and click.
3. Move the cursor to indicate the distance for creating the new object.
4. If you want a particular dimension, type it in the **Measurements** toolbar and press **Enter**.
5. If you didn't type any number, click when the new object is in the desired position.

NOTE The **Offset** tool won't allow creating one line from another, and this is why it's only active when a face or more than on line has been selected.

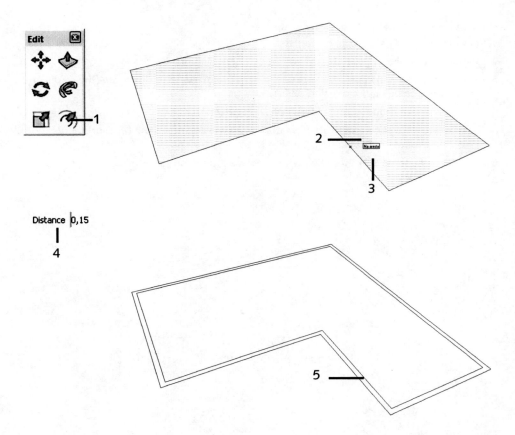

2.2 Duplication techniques

SketchUp duplication commands are quite similar to those used in other programs. The main difference is the innovative ability to make several copies from the same object.

simple duplication

1. Select the object (a line, face, or figure).

2. Choose **Edit/Copy** (*Ctrl+C*).

3. Choose **Edit/Paste** (*Ctrl+V*).

4. The copied object will automatically appear at the cursor point. Click to place it in the desired position.

duplication by moving the mouse

1. Select the object (a line, face, or figure).

2. On the **Edit toolbar**, choose the **Move** tool.

3. Press and release **Ctrl** and click on any point in the drawing to duplicate (the duplication point doesn't need to be on the selected object).

4. Move the cursor to indicate the direction of duplication.

5. If you want to duplicate with an exact distance, type a value in the **Measurements** toolbar and press **Enter** to finish duplicating the object.

6. If you didn't enter any value, click when you want to finish.

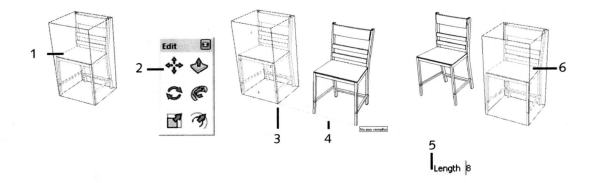

duplicate in place

1. Select the object (only works with groups or components).

2. Choose **Edit/Copy** (*Ctrl+C*).

3. Choose **Edit/Paste in Place**.

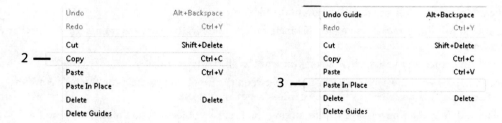

4. The copied object will automatically appear in the same place as the original. Use the **Move** tool, for example, to move the object to another location.

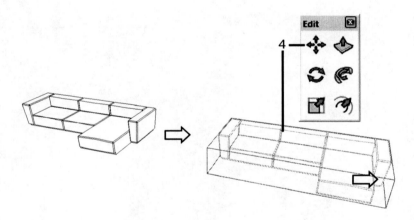

NOTE A good idea is to use this technique whenever you need to place an object in the same spot it was, but inside a group or component, for instance. To do that you must select the object and use the **Edit/Cut** (*Ctrl+X*) command.

repeated and linear duplication of an object

1. Select the object (a line, face, or figure).
2. On the **Edit toolbar**, choose the **Move** tool.
3. Press and release **Ctrl** and click on any point in the drawing to duplicate (the duplication point doesn't need to be on the selected object).
4. Move the cursor to indicate the direction of duplication.
5. If you want to duplicate with an exact distance, type a value in the **Measurements** toolbar and press **Enter**, to duplicate the object.
6. If you didn't enter any value, click when you want to stop duplication.
7. To make copies with the same spacing given between the first two objects, type the following in the **Measurements** toolbar: ***number of copies** (for example, *8).
8. To place a determined number of copies among the first two objects, type the following in the **Measurements** toolbar: **/number of copies** (for example, /8).

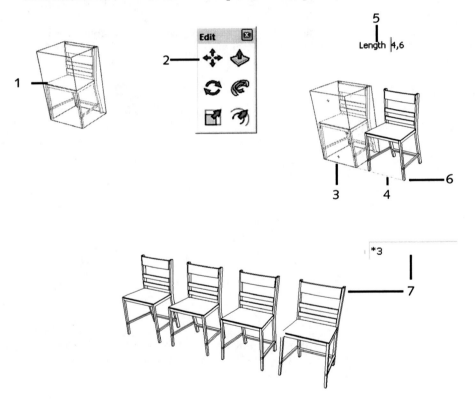

repeated and rotated duplication of an object

1. Select the object (a line, face, or figure).

2. On the **Edit toolbar,** choose the **Rotate** tool.

3. Press and release **Ctrl** and click on any point in the drawing to duplicate (the point of duplication doesn't need to be on the selected object).

4. Move the cursor to indicate the axis of the duplication and click.

5. If you want to rotate at an exact angle, type a value in the **Measurements** toolbar and press **Enter**.

6. If you didn't enter any value, click when you want to stop rotation.

7. To make copies with the same angles set for the first two objects, type the following in the **Measurements** toolbar: ***number of copies** (for example, ***3**).

8. To place a determined number of copies among the first two objects, type the following in the **Measurements** toolbar: **/number of copies** (for example, **/3**).

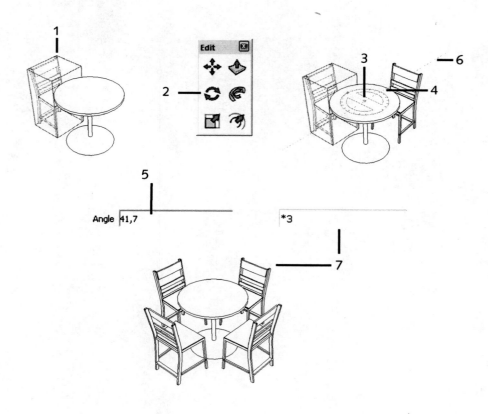

2.3 Advanced editing and creation of objects

The commands listed below depend on the existence of other objects. As a result, they can produce new objects.

how to divide lines

1. Select the line to be divided.

2. Right-click and choose the **Divide** option.

3. Type the desired number of divisions in the box and press **Enter**.

4. If you didn't enter any number, move the cursor over the line to be divided. Red blocks will appear, indicating how many divisions will exist. Click to confirm.

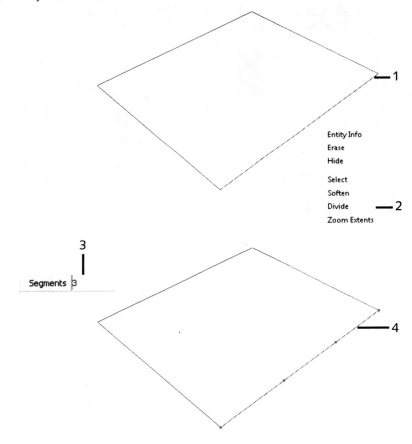

how to create an object from a profile and a path

1. Draw or use an object to be positioned perpendicularly to the starting line of the object to be created. This object will be a
   · profile reference.

2. Select all the lines (can be the edges of a polygon) that will be used as a reference for creating the object.

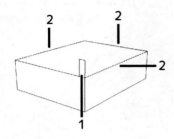

3. On the **Edit toolbar**, choose the **Follow Me** tool.

4. Click on the face of the profile object.

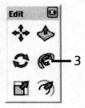

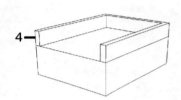

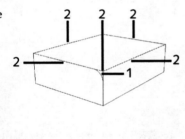

how to trim an object using Follow Me

1. Draw the profile that will be removed directly from one of the faces of the object.

2. On your project, identify the edges of the object that will be trimmed.

3. On the **Edit** toolbar, choose the **Follow Me** tool.

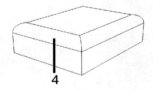

4. Click on the face to be removed.

how to edit or create objects from others, using Intersect

1. Create two or more 3D objects that intersect one another. Select them and right-click on the mouse. Choose the **Intersect Faces/With Selection** option.

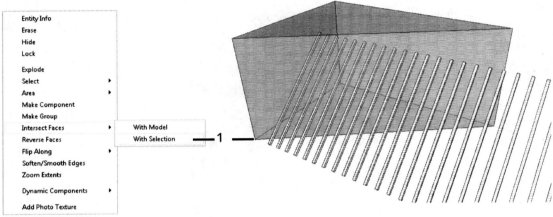

2. To see the result, delete the faces of the original objects. You'll notice that the new faces were created in the cross-section of the objects.

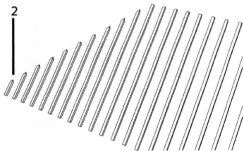

NOTE The **Intersect Faces/With Model** option causes an intersection of the selected object with all the others in contact with each other, whether selected or not.

2.4 Drawing roof faces

To draw a roof, you'll need to draw it as a plan. To lift it, use the **Move** tool. You can create practically any roof with this technique.

how to create a roof faces

1. Create the roof drawing as a plan.

2. Select the points and/or roof lines that will be on top (or represent the ridge).

3. On the **Edit toolbar**, choose the **Move** tool.

4. Move the cursor to raise the roof height and click to stop.

5. If you want to set an exact height value, type it in the **Measurements** toolbar and press **Enter**, to finish moving the ridge.

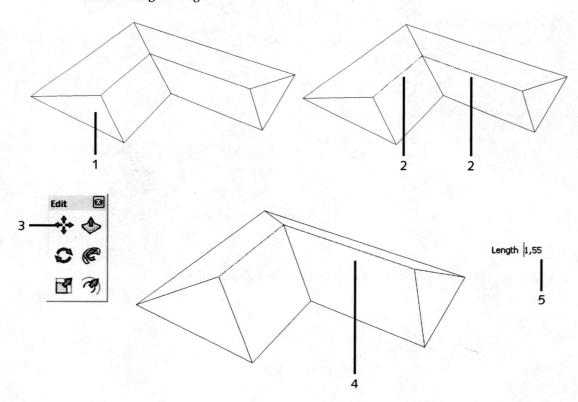

NOTE You can use the roof geometry as a reference to build an entire roof structure. To do that we recommend you download a free add-on called 1001bit Standard. Among a lot of nice tools, you'll find some advanced tools for creating an entire roof structure. Visit **http://www.1001bit.com** and take a look at it. For now, it's not available in the Extensions Warehouse.

2.5 Placing 3D texts

SketchUp has a tool that can convert any text into a 3D drawing, which can be placed in any position on the project. The converted 3D text becomes a group of lines and faces, so you can use tools like **Push/Pull** and **Follow Me**, among others.

to transform a text into a 3D drawing

1. On the **Construction** toolbar, choose the **3D Text** tool.

2. Configure these options:

   a. Here, enter the text you want converted;
   b. Choose the font and style you will use;
   c. In the **Align** field, choose the text alignment as it relates to the cursor, just after clicking **OK**;
   d. In **Height**, set the height of the mid-section of the text;
   e. Indicate if the text will have faces (**Form Filled**) and if they will be **Extruded**.
3. Click on **Place**.

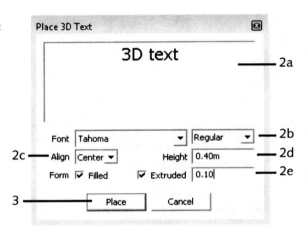

4. Move the cursor over the drawing to choose the text position. Click to finish.

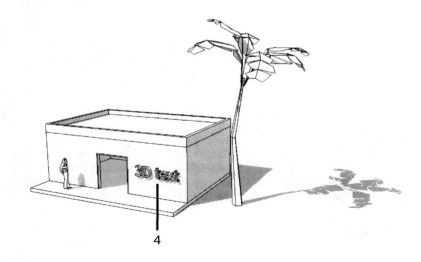

2.6 Drawing aids

Drawing aids are elements that facilitate the creation of objects. Accessories called **Inferences** are tips that appear on the screen, indicating centers, ends of lines, and edges of objects; there are also the **Guides** and **Guide Points**, which permit construction of objects at a distance from each other, or in different directions than usual; one also can use the drawing's own **Axis**, which can be altered at your convenience.

how to understand SketchUp Inferences

Inferences, or hints, exist to indicate important geometric points (centers, endpoints, general alignment) of objects in an easy and innovative way. For a tip to appear, simply hover the cursor over the desired place (for example, if you move the cursor close to the center of a line, the **Midpoint** tip will appear). The screens tips can be divided into **Point Inferences** and **Linear Inferences**.

Point Inferences:

1. **Endpoint:** Upon passing the cursor over the end of a line or arc, the **Endpoint** tip will appear beside a green circle.
2. **Midpoint:** Upon passing the cursor over the midpoint of a line or edge of a polygon, the **Midpoint** tip will appear beside a teal circle.
3. **On Edge:** Upon passing the cursor over the edge of an object, the **On Edge** tip will appear beside a red circle.
4. **On Face:** Upon passing the cursor over the face of an object, the **On Face** tip will appear beside a blue circle.
5. **Half Circle:** This tip appears when, while making an arc, you near a half circle with the bow.

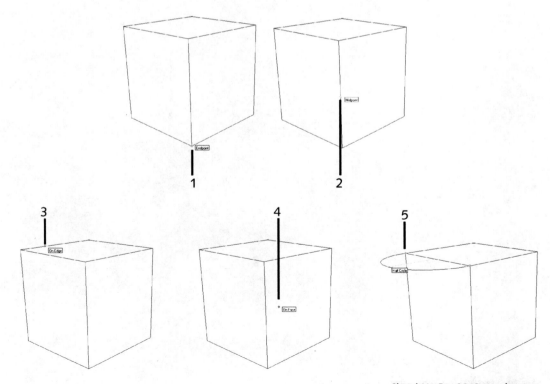

Linear Inferences:

1. **On Axis**: Upon making a line and moving it in the area, the **On Axis** tip will appear when your line is placed on one of the drawing's axes. A colored line with a text will appear; the color depends on the axis represented.

2. **From Point**: If you pass the cursor over a point and move it away in the direction of an axis, the **From Point** tip will appear. A dashed, colored line will appear with a text; the color depends on the axis represented.

3. **Perpendicular to Edge**: This tip appears below a purple line, when trying to draw a line that is perpendicular to the edge of an object.

4. **Parallel to Edge**: Also appears as a purple line, when trying to draw a line that is parallel to the edge of an object.

5. **Tangent**: This tip appears when you make an arc that begins at the point of another arc. When the second arc is positioned in the tangent of the first, the **Tangent** tip appears.

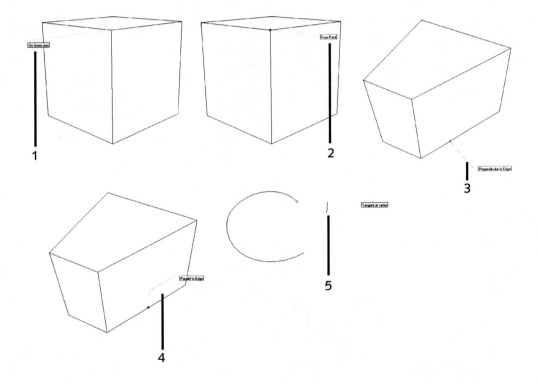

why and how to create Guides and Guide Points

Certain types of objects are very difficult, sometimes impossible, to create using only the traditional tools in SketchUp. The guides are drawing components that help to create several objects, and can be made to temporarily disappear, or even be deleted, without interfering with the project.

guide point

1. On the **Construction** toolbar, choose the **Tape Measure** tool.
2. Click on a corner (group of lines) of an object.
3. Move the cursor to indicate the direction in which to create the guide point.
4. If you want to set an exact distance, type a value in the **Measurements** toolbar and press **Enter** to finish placing the point.
5. If you didn't enter any value, click when you want to finish inserting the guide point. Notice that SketchUp draws a dashed line that can also be used as a guide.

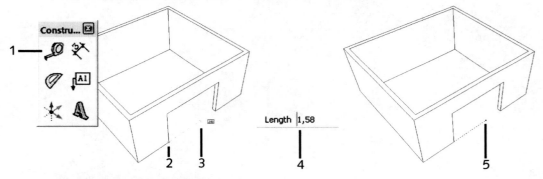

guide – parallel to an object edge (line)

1. On the **Construction** toolbar, choose the **Tape Measure** tool.
2. Click on the edge (line) of an object.
3. Move the cursor perpendicularly to the edge to indicate the distance at which to create the guide.
4. If you want to set an exact distance, type a value in the **Measurements** toolbar and press **Enter** to finish the line.
5. If you didn't enter any value, click when you want to finish inserting the guide. Notice that SketchUp draws an infinitely long dashed line.

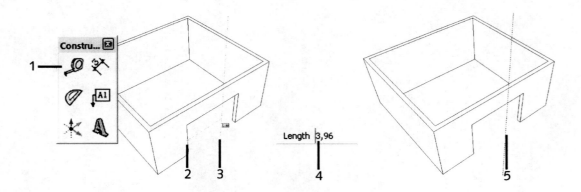

guide – angular in relation to an object

1. On the **Construction** toolbar, choose the **Protractor** tool.

2. Click on any point of the drawing. This can be a corner, edge, a point on a face, or even a place where there is no object.

3. Move the cursor to indicate the angle at which to create the construction line.

4. If you want to set an exact angle, type a value in the **Measurements** toolbar and press **Enter** to finish placing the line.

5. If you didn't enter any value, click when you want to finish inserting the guide. Notice that SketchUp draws an infinitely long dashed line.

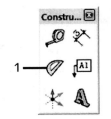

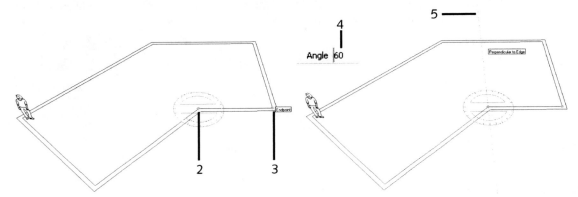

how to force the direction to draw faster

You can draw faster if, while drawing, you "force" the direction of the tracer accompanying either of the axes. Try the following:

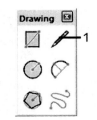

1. On the **Drawing** toolbar, choose the **Line** tool.

2. Click the starting point of the line and move the cursor in any direction.

3. If you press the **right arrow key**, the line will be forced out in the red direction.

4. If you press the **left arrow key**, the line will be forced out in the green direction.

5. If you press the **up arrow key** or the **down arrow key**, the line will be forced out in the blue direction.

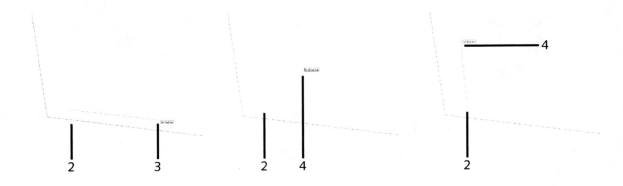

how to use axes in SketchUp

If you need to draw several objects which are fixed to a different plane than the original working plane, use the **Axes** tool to alter the drawing axes origin and orientation and draw more easily.

If you wish, you can quickly return the working plane to the original position.

1. On the **Construction** toolbar, choose the **Axes** tool.

2. Move the cursor to indicate the point of origin of the new working plane. Click to confirm.

3. Move the cursor to indicate the direction of the red axis. Click to confirm.

4. Move the cursor to indicate the direction of the green axis. Click to confirm.

5. The new working plane has been set, and the blue axis will appear perpendicularly to the other two.

> **NOTE** To return the working plane to its original position, click the right button over the axes and select **Reset**.

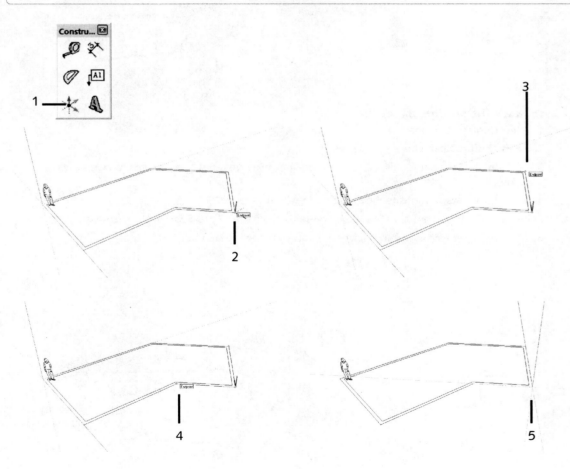

2.7 Sectioning objects

Some tridimensional objects are more easily understood when sectioned. SketchUp has a very simple, practical and elegant way to show them, with a tool called **Section Plane**.

to place a section plane

1. On the **Section** toolbar, choose the **Section Plane** tool.
2. A section plane (presented as a green block) will appear. Move it and notice how it sticks to the faces of the objects.
3. When the section plane gets fixed as you wish, click to confirm.

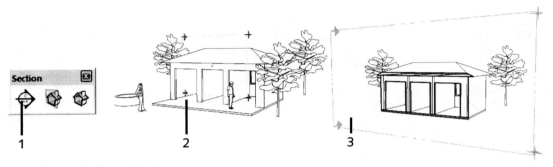

to move the section plane

1. Select the section plane.
2. On the **Edit** toolbar, choose the **Move** tool.
3. Click on any point of the drawing and move it (the move point doesn't need to be on the section plane).
4. Move the cursor to indicate the direction in which to move.
5. If you want, type a value in the **Measurements** toolbar and press **Enter**, to execute the movement.
6. If you didn't enter any value, click when you want to stop moving.

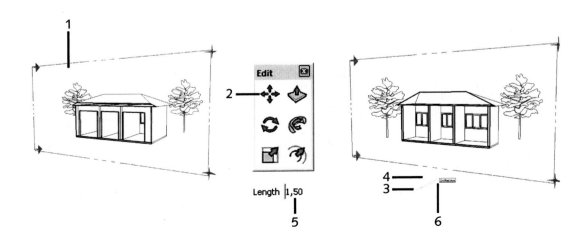

to rotate a section plane

1. Select the section plane.

2. On the **Edit** toolbar, choose the **Rotate** tool.

3. Click on the point that will be the center of the axis of rotation (this center should not be in the section plane).

4. Move the cursor to indicate the spin of the axis of rotation.

5. If you want, type a value in the **Measurements** toolbar and press **Enter**, to execute the section plane rotation.

6. If you didn't enter any value, click when the spin is desirable.

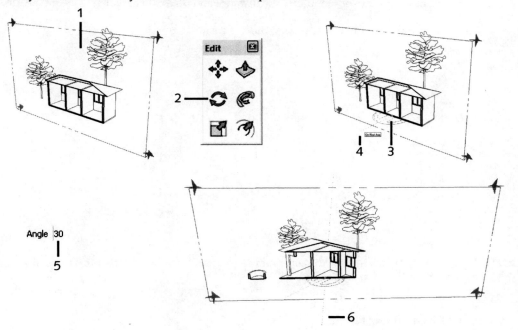

other interesting options

1. To show or hide a section plane, select it and choose **View/Section Planes** menu.

2. To show or hide the cut part of the object, select it and choose **View/Section Cuts** menu.

3. To change the direction of a section plane, right-click and choose **Reverse**.

4. Right-click over the section plane and use the **Align View** command. By doing this, SketchUp places the viewer perpendicularly to the section cut.

5. If you want to make a new drawing from the resulting section plane lines, right-click and choose **Create Group from Slice**. Next, move the newly created group to a different area and continue drawing from there.

2.8 Dimensions and annotations

Even though the program isn't designed for creating blueprints, SketchUp has good tools for adding dimensions and annotations. The objects created with these tools are native 3D, and are always associated with the figured object; a characteristic that's usually found in sophisticated CAD programs.

to figure an object

1. On the **Construction** toolbar, choose the **Dimension** tool.
2. Move the cursor over the line to measure.
3. Click and move the cursor to indicate the distance and direction at which to create the dimension line.
4. Click when you want to finish inserting the dimension line.

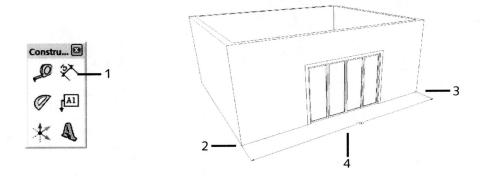

> **NOTE** To alter the characteristics of dimension lines, choose **Window/Model Info/Dimensions** menu. See more about this on page **249**.

how to edit a dimension line

1. Select the dimension line you want to edit (**a**), right-click and choose **Entity Info** (**b**).

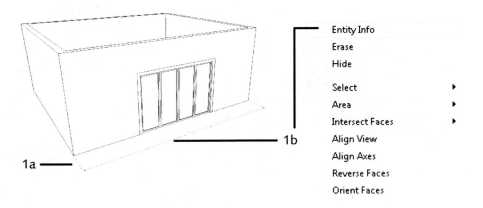

2. Adjust the following options:

a. Click this button to choose the dimension line color;

b. **Align to screen**: This option makes your dimension texts always appear facing the viewer.

c. **Align to dimension**: Click this option to fix the text to the dimension, according to your position on the drawing;

d. **Hidden**: Hide the dimension, so that it can only be shown again if you use the **View/ Hidden Geometry** menu;

e. **Layer**: Choose the dimension layer;

f. **Change Font**: Click this button to set the dimension font;

g. **Text Position**: Choose if the text is to be centered or placed beside the dimension (left or right);

h. **Endpoints**: Click to choose the appearance of the dimension line endpoints.

3. After making all adjustments, close the window.

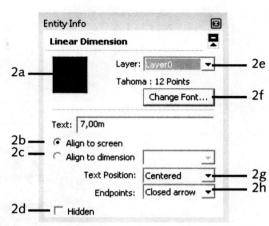

NOTE To alter default dimension settings for SketchUp, go to **Window/Model Info/Dimension**. See more on page **249**.

placing annotations in the project

1. On the **Construction** toolbar, choose the **Text** tool.

2. Click the point, line or face on which you want to make an annotation.

3. Move the cursor to position the text in the drawing.

4. Click to finish.

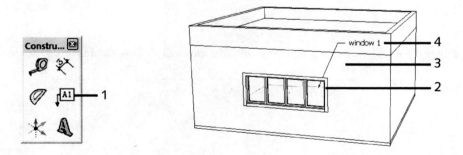

NOTE 1 If you click a point, SketchUp automatically places its coordinates. If it's on a line, it shows the length. If on a face, the area is shown.

NOTE 2 If you click on an empty area of the drawing, SketchUp places a floating text, separate from any object.

how to edit an annotation

1. Select the text you want to edit (**a**), right-click and choose **Entity Info** (**b**).

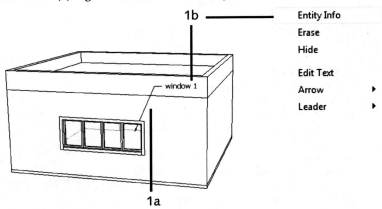

2. In the window that opens, adjust the following options:

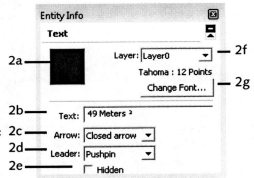

  a. Click this button to choose a color for the annotation;

  b. **Text**: Enter a text that will appear as an annotation;

  c. **Arrow**: Choose the type of arrow that will point out the notated object;

  d. **Leader**: Configure the leader line seen by the viewer as **View Based**, or if it is read as a **Pushpin**;

  e. **Hidden**: Hide the leader line so that it is only shown again if you use the **View/Hidden Geometry** menu;

  f. **Layer**: Choose the annotation layer;

  g. **Change Font...**: Click this button to set the font.

3. After making all adjustments, close the window if preferred.

NOTE To change defaults for inserting notes in SketchUp, choose **Window/Model Info/Dimension** menu. See more on page **249**.

Chapter highlights

Duplication (p. 48)

Select the object and choose **Edit/Copy** menu; after that, Choose **Edit/Paste** menu; the copied object will appear on the cursor point. Click to place it in the desired position.

By moving the mouse (p. 48)

Select the object; on the **Edit toolbar**, choose the **Move** tool; press and release **Ctrl** and click on any point in the drawing to duplicate; move the cursor to indicate the direction in which to duplicate. Click when you want to stop.

Repeated and linear duplication of an object (p. 50)

Select the object and, on the **Edit toolbar**, choose the **Move** tool; press and release **Ctrl**; click on any point in the drawing to duplicate; move the cursor to indicate the direction in which to duplicate. Click when you want to stop. To make copies with the same spacing given between the first two objects, type the following in the **Measurements** toolbar: ***number of copies** (for example, *8).

Repeated and rotated duplication of an object (p. 52)

Select the object, and on the **Edit toolbar**, choose the **Rotate** tool; press and release **Ctrl** and click on any point in the drawing to duplicate; move the cursor to indicate the duplication axis and click; click again when you want to stop the rotation; to make copies with the same angles given to the first two objects, type the following in the **Measurements** toolbar: ***number of copies** (for example, *8).

How to divide lines (p. 52)

Select the line to be divided, click the right button and choose the **Divide** option; type the desired number of divisions in the box and press **Enter**.

How to create an object from a profile and a Follow Me path (p. 53)

Draw or use an object that is positioned perpendicularly to the starting line of the object to be created. This object will be a profile reference; select all the lines (can be the edges of a polygon) that will be used as a reference for creating the object; choose the **Follow Me** tool on the **Edit** menu, and click on the face of the profile object.

New objects using Intersect (p. 54)

Create two or more 3D objects that intersect. Select and right-click them. Choose the **Intersect/With Selection** option. To see the result, delete the faces from the original objects. You'll notice new faces were created where the objects intersect.

Drawing roof faces (p. 56)

To draw a roof, you need to draw it as a plan. To lift it, use the **Move** tool. You can create practically any roof with this technique.

Placing 3D text (p. 57)

SketchUp has a tool that can convert text into a 3D drawing, which can be placed in any position on the project. The converted 3D text becomes a group of lines and faces, and you can use tools like **Push/Pull** and **Follow Me** on them, among others.

Guides (p. 59)

Guides are elements of drawing that assist in the creation of various objects which can be made to disappear temporarily, or even be deleted, without interfering with the project.

Sectioning objects

Place a section plane (p. 62)

On the **Sections** toolbar, choose the **Section Plane** tool; a section plane will appear. Move it, and notice how it sticks to the faces of objects; when the section plane is fixed the way you want, click to confirm.

To move the section plane (p. 62)

Select the section plane; on the **Edit toolbar**, click on the **Move** tool; click on any point of the drawing to move it, and move the cursor to indicate the movement direction; click to stop.

Dimensions and annotations

To figure an object (p. 64)

Choose the **Dimension** tool and move the cursor over the line you want to figure; click and move it to indicate the distance and direction at which to create it; click to finish inserting the dimension line.

Placing annotations in a project (p. 65)

Choose the **Text** tool and click on a point, line or face that you want to rotate; move the cursor to position the text on the drawing and click to finish.

Suggested activities

Ex. 01 – Offset

1. Open the **Cap02_Ex01.skp** file.

2. Use the **Offset** tool and type 6" or 0.15m, as shown in *figs. 04a* and *04b*.

3. Use the **Push/Pull** and type 118" or 3m, as in *figs. 05a* and *05b*.

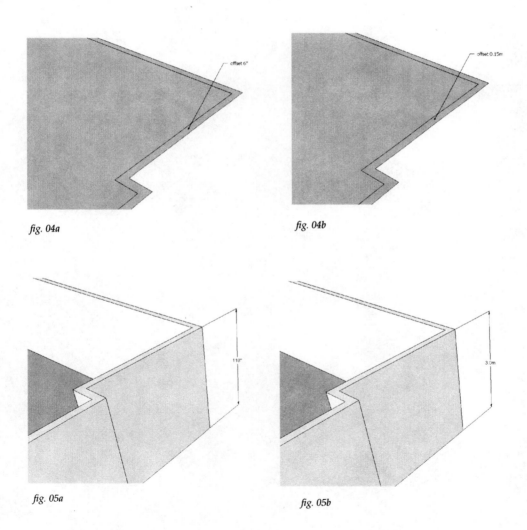

fig. 04a

fig. 04b

fig. 05a

fig. 05b

Ex. 02 – Rotate, move, and scale

1. Open the **Cap02_Ex02.skp** file.

2. Rotate the table 90°, starting from the indicated endpoint (*fig. 06*).

3. Move the table 70" or 1,8m, as in *fig. 07*.

4. Scale the table to 106" or 2,7m, as in *fig. 08*.

fig. 06

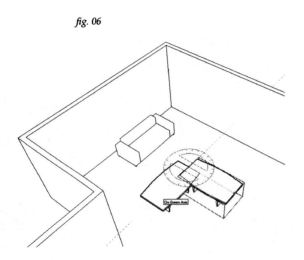

fig. 07

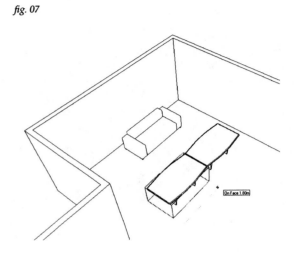

fig. 08

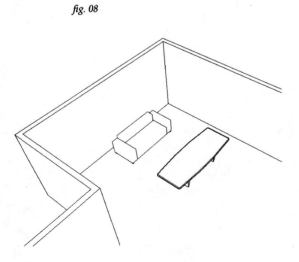

Ex. 03 – Linear and rotated duplication

1. Open the **Cap02_Ex03.skp** file.

2. Use the **Move** tool to place 3 more armchairs, spaced at 47" or 1,2m (*figs. 09, 10a* and *10b*).

3. With the **Rotate** tool, place 3 more chairs around the table, as shown in *figs. 11a* and *11b*.

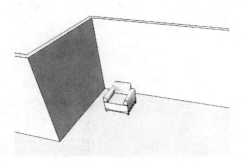

fig. 09

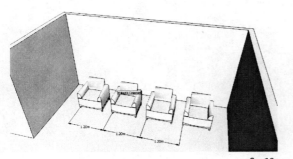

fig. 10a

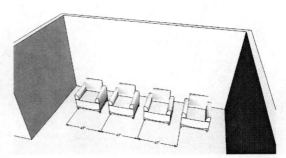

fig. 10b

fig. 11a

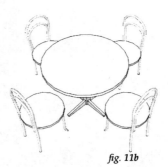

fig. 11b

Ex. 04 – Guides, Offset, and Push/Pull

1. Open the **Cap02_Ex04.skp** file.

2. Use the **Tape Measure** tool to make the guides indicated in *figs. 12a* and *12b*.

3. With the **Offset** tool, draw the marking indicated on the wall (*fig. 13a* and *13b*).

4. Use the **Push/Pull** tool to make the door and window openings, and to create the shelf, measuring 16" or 0,40m (*fig. 14a* and *14b*).

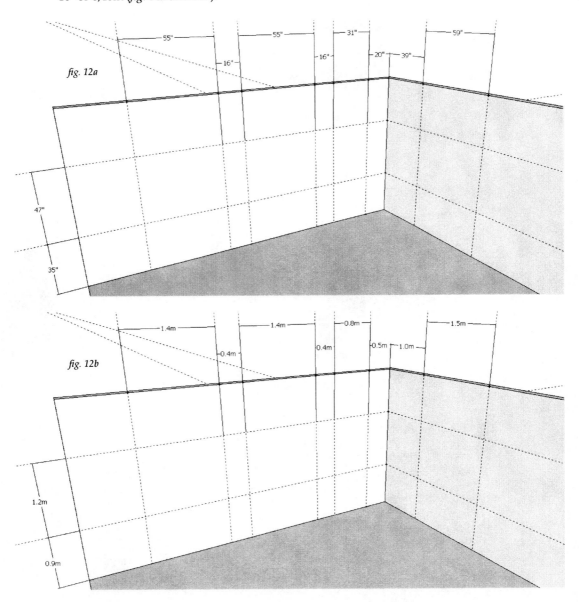

fig. 12a

fig. 12b

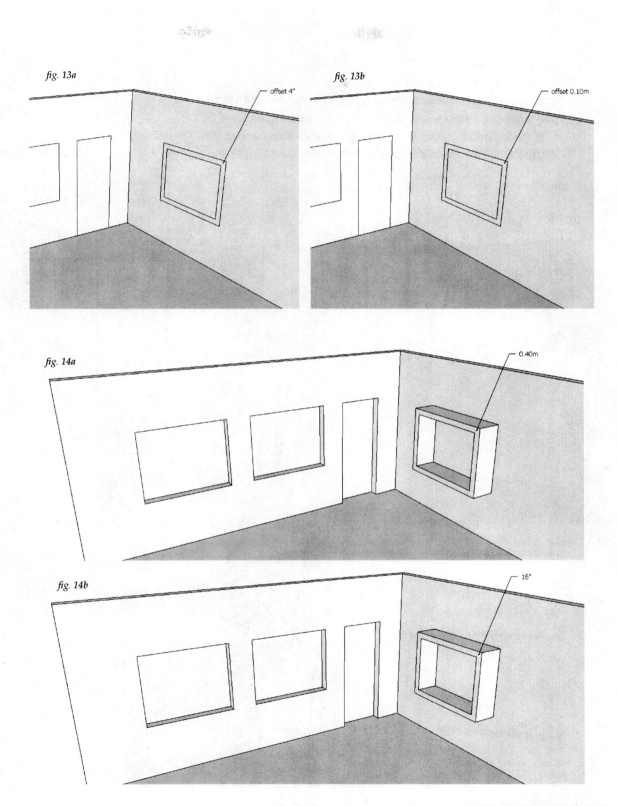

fig. 13a — offset 4"

fig. 13b — offset 0.10m

fig. 14a — 0.40m

fig. 14b — 16"

Ex. 05 – Follow Me

1. Open the **Cap02_Ex05.skp** file.
2. Draw the profile of the crown molding, as in *figs. 15a* and *15b*.
3. Use the **Follow Me** tool to create the crown molding, as in *fig. 16*.
4. With the **Arc** tool, draw an arc on top of the shelf on the wall (*figs. 17a* and *17b*).
5. Use the **Follow Me** tool to round off the entire shelf (*figs. 18* and *19*).

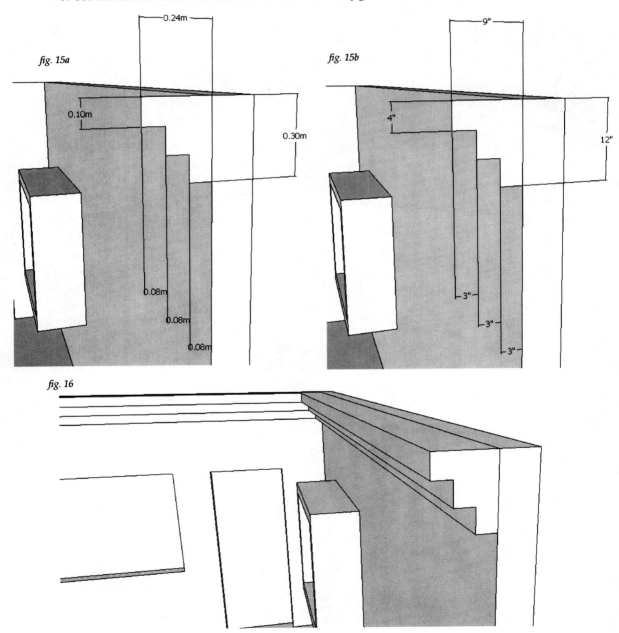

fig. 15a

fig. 15b

fig. 16

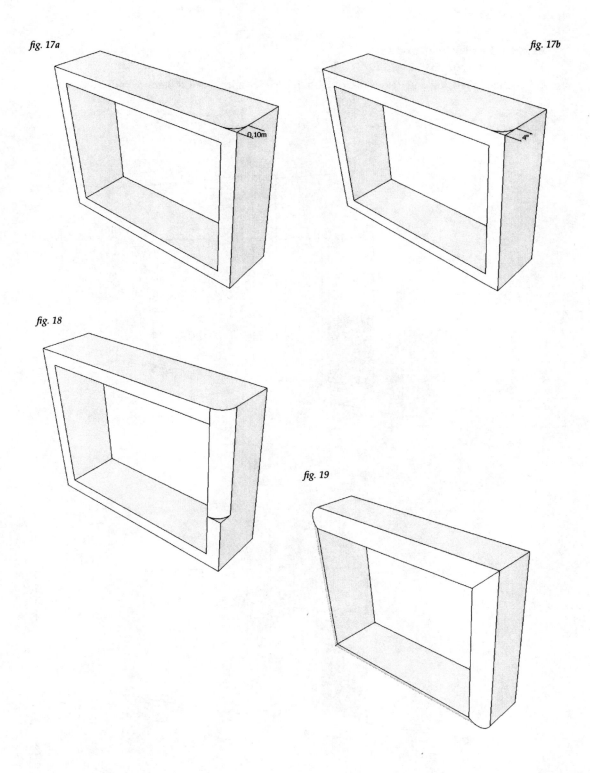

fig. 17a

0.10m

fig. 17b

4"

fig. 18

fig. 19

Ex. 06 – Leader lines and text

1. Open the **Cap02_Ex06.skp** file.

2. Use the **Dimension** and **Text** tools to create the leader lines and annotations indicated in *figs. 20a* and *20b*.

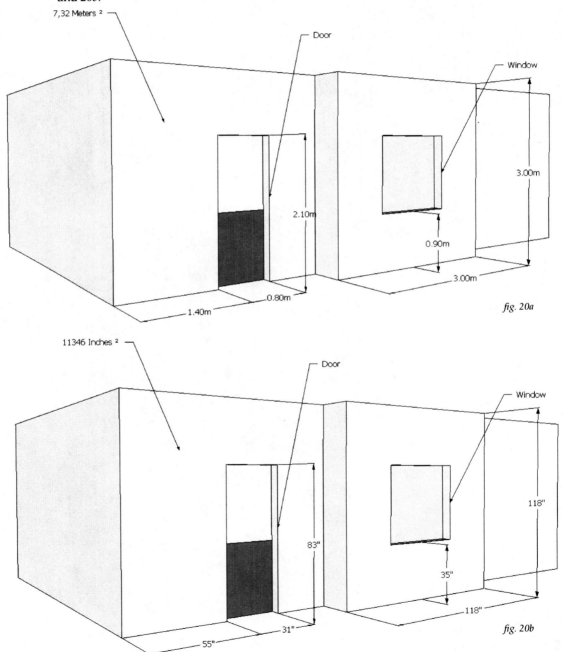

fig. 20a

fig. 20b

Ex. 07 – Roof

1. Open the **Cap02_Ex07.skp** file.

2. Use the **Line** tool to create the roof as a plan drawing, as seen in *fig. 21a*.

3. Select the lines that represent the ridge and lift them to 59" or 1,5m with the **Move** tool (*fig. 21b*).

4. Make the roof a group and place it on the house, aligning the rear point of the roof with the rear point of the house. Next, move the roof 18" or 0,45m away from the house, in both directions (*figs. 22a* and *22b*).

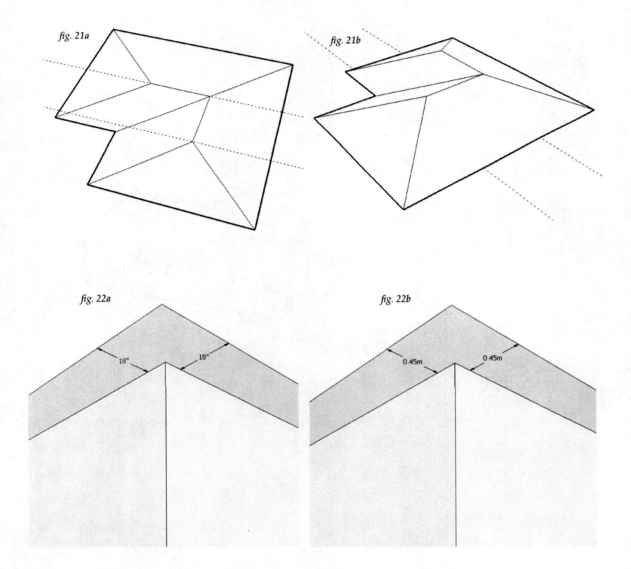

fig. 21a

fig. 21b

fig. 22a

fig. 22b

Ex. 08 – To section an object

1. Open the **Cap02_Ex08.skp** file.

2. Use the **Section Plane** tool to create a section plane, as in *fig. 23*.

3. With the **Move** tool, choose the position of the sections, as shown in *fig. 24*.

4. If preferred, hide the section plane, by deactivating **View/Section Planes**.

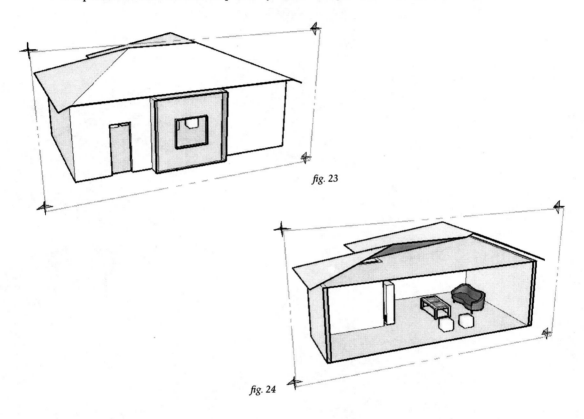

fig. 23

fig. 24

Now the project is complete, and the time has come to improve the presentation. I need to know the best application techniques for

shadows, colors, and textures

In addition to being a powerful and easy to use 3D modeler, SketchUp has great presentation resources. It's possible to adjust shadow projection for any hour, configure colors and transparencies in objects, apply textures, configure the display style of lines, and much more.

What you'll read in this chapter

3.1 Basic display options

3.2 How to use styles

3.3 Colors and materials (textures) – Windows version

3.4 Colors and materials (textures) – Mac version

3.5 How to create objects with the aid of an image

3.6 How to create objects with Match Photo

3.1 Basic display options

Working just a little with SketchUp allows you to see its particular way of showing objects. Even if you don't apply textures (which we'll see later), the presentation results in SketchUp are of excellent quality.

different display types

On the **Face Style** menu, choose from among the display options:

1. **Wireframe**, in which all the object lines are shown, as if made of wire.
2. **Hidden Line**, paints all faces with the background color, which is defined on the **Edit** tab; check page **85**, item **5a**. This display type also hides the lines that aren't visible in the current viewer position.
3. **Shaded**, displays the faces with their primary colors, in addition to their own shadows, caused by the position of the sun.
4. **Shaded with Textures**, displays faces with colors, textures, and shading.
5. **Monochrome**, similar to **Hidden Line**, however, uses SketchUp default colors for display.

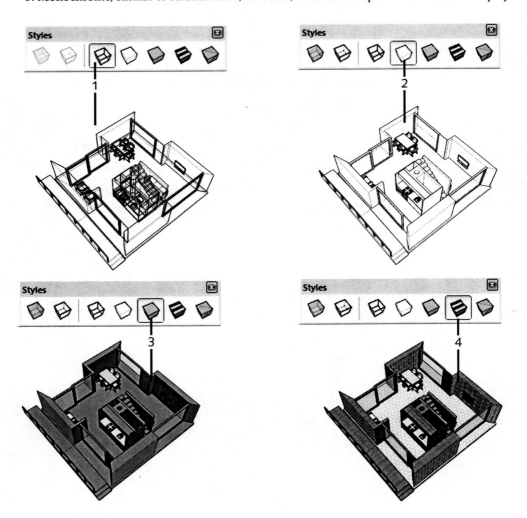

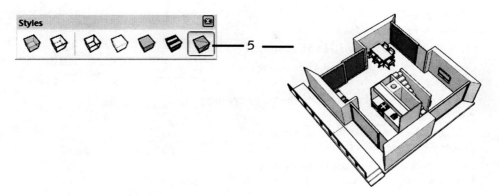

X-Ray mode

The X-Ray mode adds a transparent effect to the display types previously mentioned (except **Wireframe**).

1. On the **Face Style** menu, choose the **X-Ray** button and observe the effect.

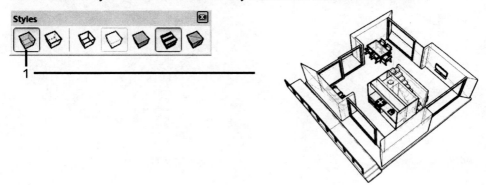

Back Edges mode

The **Back Edges** mode applies a dashed effect on the hidden edges from the view of the observer.

1. On the **Face Style** menu, choose the **Back Edges** button and observe the effect.

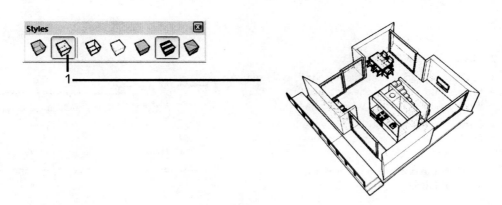

configure shadows

1. Choose **Window/Shadows**.

2. Click the box to **Display/Hide Shadows**.

3. Choose the preferred hour in **Time**, using the bar or typing it in the field to the side.

4. Choose the preferred **Date**, using the bar or typing it in the field to the side.

5. In **Light**, adjust the amount of light applied directly on the faces of the objects.

6. On the **Dark** bar, adjust the intensity of the shadows being projected.

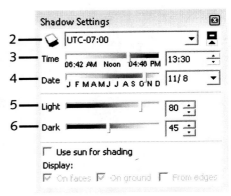

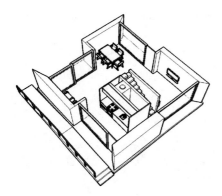

option 2 disabled

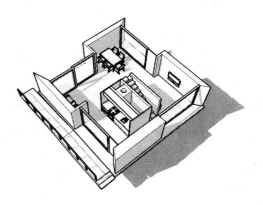

option 2 enabled

configure fog

1. Choose **Window/Fog**.

Layers
Outliner
Scenes

Shadows
Fog ——————1

2. Click the box to **Display Fog**.

3. In **Distance**, adjust the distance from where the fog will start (**a**), and the distance from where the fog will cover as a whole (**b**).

4. Click the indicated button to make it so the fog has the same color used in the project background.

5. Deselect the box indicated in **4** and click in the indicated area to choose a color for the fog.

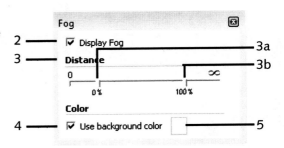

3.2 How to use styles

In addition to the basic configurations mentioned earlier, SketchUp allows other changes to the display settings of your project. Changes to line styles, face styles, sky and ground settings can be made. It's also possible to insert watermarks and configure the display style for SketchUp tools. You can make all these adjustments and save them as a style. You can create new styles, or just use those that come with the program.

how to use a style
1. Choose **Window/Styles**.
2. Click the **Select** tab.
3. In the dropdown list, select the folder that contains the style you want to apply.
4. Click on the style and observe the result.

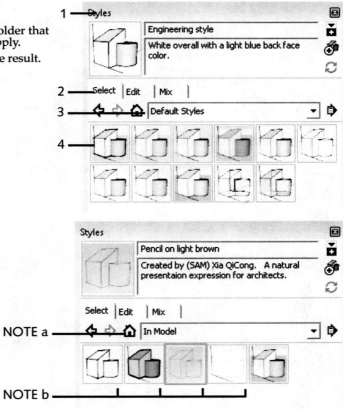

NOTE Each time you choose a style, SketchUp places it in your file. In the **Styles** window, click on the house icon button (**a**), to see which styles are in your file (**b**).

how to create a style

1. Choose **Window/Styles**.

2. Click the **Edit** tab.

3. Click the indicated icon to activate line configurations, called **Edges**. Configure the following options:

a. **Edges**: Enable or disable the edge enhancement options;

b. **Back Edges**: Enable or disable the visibility of hidden dashed edges;

c. **Profiles**: Thickens lines that separate the model from the background, as well as the edges of objects that, in the current camera view, make no boundary with any other;

d. **Depth Cue**: Thickens the lines that are closer to the viewer;

e. **Extension**: Augments the edges to beyond their boundaries;

f. **Endpoints**: Thickens the edges at their junctions;

g. **Jitter**: Applies a blurred effect to the edges.

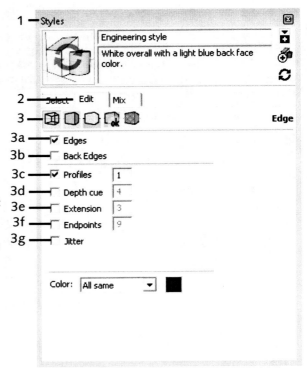

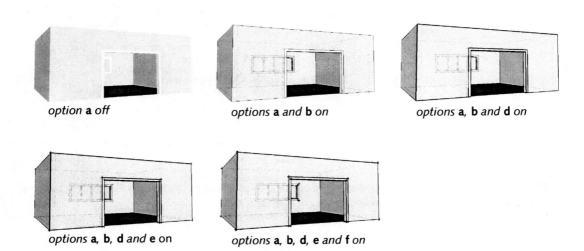

*option **a** off*   *options **a** and **b** on*   *options **a**, **b** and **d** on*

*options **a**, **b**, **d** and **e** on*   *options **a**, **b**, **d**, **e** and **f** on*

4. Click the indicated icon to activate the face configurations:

a. **Front Color**: Click to alter the default color for the front sides of faces;

b. **Back Color**: Alter the default color for the back sides of faces;

c. **Style**: Configure the display style of faces;

d. **X-ray**: Enable or disable the X-Ray effect;

e. **Enable Transparency**: Enable or disable the transparency effect;

f. **Transparency quality**: Control the quality of transparency.

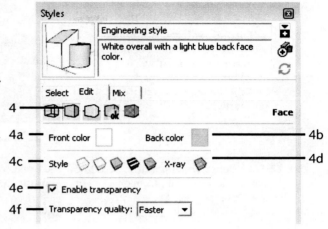

5. Click the indicated icon to activate the screen background configurations:

a. **Background**: Click to alter the color of the screen background;

b. **Sky**: Alter the sky color. This will supersede the color chosen for the background;

c. **Ground**: Alter the ground color. This will supersede the color chosen for the background. Transparency controls the opacity of the ground color;

d. **Show ground from below**: Continue showing the ground color even when the viewer is below ground level.

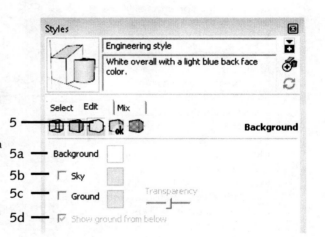

NOTE For a better understanding about how the background, sky, ground, model space and watermarks are related, check the item, **relationship between sky, ground, model space and other style features**, page 88.

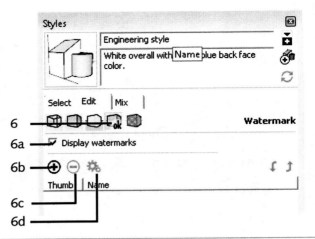

6. Click the indicated icon to activate the watermark configurations:

a. **Display watermarks**: Enable or disable the watermark options;
b. **+**: Add a watermark;
c. **-**: Remove a watermark;
d. Edit the selected watermark properties.

> **NOTE** For a better understanding about how the background, sky, ground, model space and watermarks are related, check the item, **relationship between sky, ground, model space and other style features**, page 88.

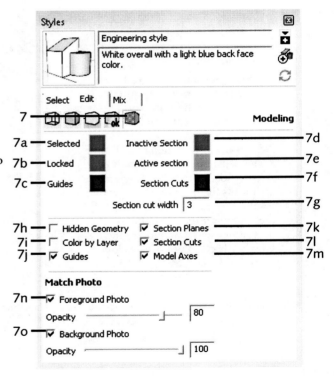

7. Click on the indicated icon to configure the appearance of the modeling tools. Configure the following options:

a. **Selected**: Choose a color that identifies a selected object;
b. **Locked**: Choose a color that identifies a locked object;
c. **Guides**: Set a color to identify the guides;
d. **Inactive Section**: Choose a color to identify inactive section planes;
e. **Active section**: Set a color to identify active section planes;
f. **Section Cuts**: Choose a color that identifies an active section cut;
g. **Section cut width**: Adjust the width of a section cut;
h. **Hidden Geometry**: Enable or disable the hidden objects option;
i. **Color by Layer**: Enable or disable the option to color objects according to their layer;
j. **Guides**: Enable or disable the appearance of guides;
k. **Section Planes**: Enable or disable the appearance of section planes;
l. **Section Cuts**: Enable or disable the appearance of section cuts;
m. **Model Axes**: Enable or disable the appearance of the drawing axes;
n. **Foreground Photo**: Enable or disable, and adjust the opacity of the model, when viewed over a scene that contains a matched photo;
o. **Background Photo**: Enable or disable, and adjust the opacity of a photo used for creating a model in the matched photo mode.

8. After configuring the options, name the style (**a**), then click the indicated button (**b**).

9. Click on the **Select** tab and observe the style you created.

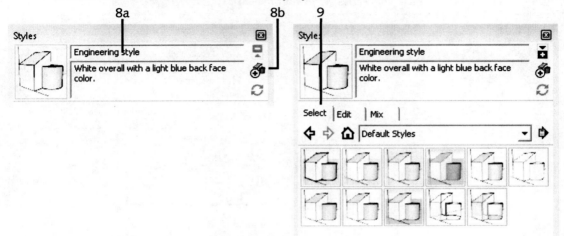

how to create a style by mixing items from other styles

The **Mix** function, in the **Styles** window, allows you to create a style by mixing the settings of several others. You can, for example, use the background from one style and the line configurations from another, etc. After mixing, you can create a new style.

1. Choose **Window/Styles**.

2. Click the indicated button to open the secondary pane.

3. Click on the **Mix** tab.

4. From the indicated dropdown list, select the folder containing the style you want to use as a reference.

5. Click on the style and drag the cursor to one of the fields above: **Edge Settings, Face Settings, Background Settings, Watermark Settings**, and **Modeling Settings**. Observe the result in the drawing window.

6. You can do this as many times as you like until you find a configuration that suits you best. If you prefer, save the settings as a new style.

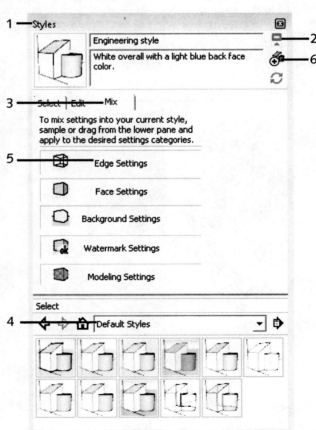

> **NOTE** Each time you choose a style, SketchUp places it in your file. In the **Styles** window, click on the indicated button (**a**) to see what styles are in your file (**b**).

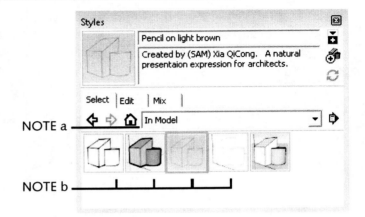

NOTE a

NOTE b

relationship between sky, ground, model space and other style features

In the graph below you can learn how background, sky, ground, model space and watermarks are organized; that way you can take more advantage of the style features.

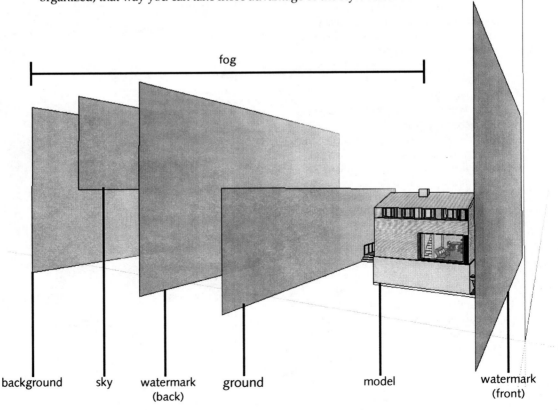

3.3 Colors and materials (textures) – Windows version

In addition to painting with solid colors, you can use SketchUp's vast materials library (textures). If the library doesn't have the image you want, choose from any on your computer. You can also alter the base image, adding a color or changing its opacity.

to apply a material to an object

1. Choose **Window/Materials**.

2. Click on **Select** to choose one of the texture libraries.

3. Select the library containing the texture you want from the drop list.

4. Click on the texture you want to use to paint.

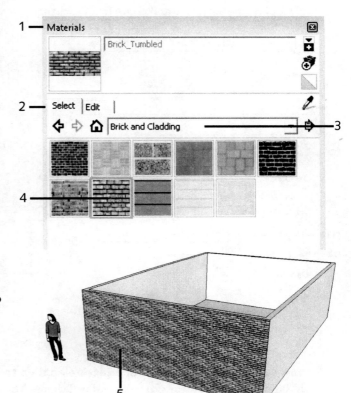

5. Click on the surface you want to paint.

how to edit a material being used in a model

1. Choose **Window/Materials**.

2. Click on the image of the material to be edited.

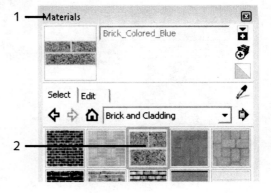

3. Click on the **Edit** tab.

4. Choose a color system (RGB, HSB, HLS or Color Wheel), and find the color you want to use for mixing with the texture.

5. Enter the width and/or height desired (**a** and **b**) for the texture size. Click on the chain (**c**) to enable or disable proportional relation between the width and height of the texture.

6. If you'd like, alter the opacity of the material, by using the **Opacity** control.

7. Click on the **Select** tab and notice that the changes have already taken effect on the object.

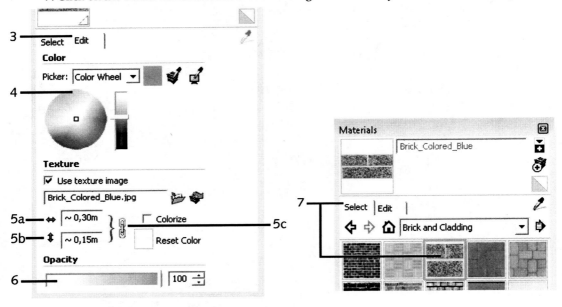

how to create a material from a texture applied to a face

1. Right-click on the texture to be copied and choose **Make Unique Texture**.

2. Choose **Window/Materials** and notice that a new texture has been created. The name of the texture is the same as before with a **#1** added.

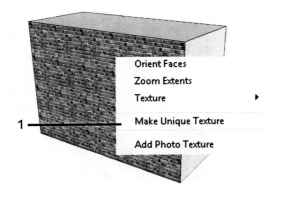

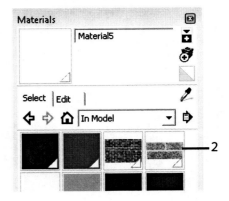

how to create a new material

1. Choose **Window/Materials**.
2. Click on the **Create Material** button.

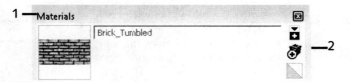

3. Use this field to give the material a name.
4. Choose a color system (RGB, HSB, HLS or Color Wheel), and find the color you want to use for mixing the texture.
5. If you want to use an image as the base of the material, click on **Use texture image** (**a**), then click on the folder icon (**b**).
6. Select the image file (JPG, BMP, TIF, etc.) (**a**) and click on **Open** (**b**).

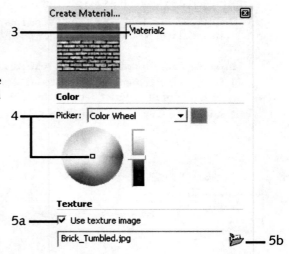

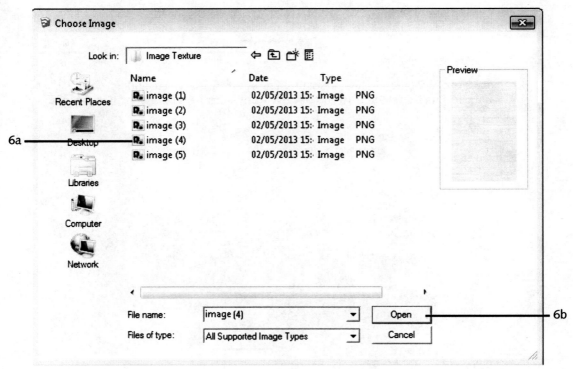

7. Enter the desired width and/or height (**a** and **b**) for the texture size. Click the chain (**c**) to lock or unlock the aspect ratio between the width and height of the texture.

8. If you prefer, alter the opacity of the material by using the **Opacity** control.

9. Click **OK** to save the active material. This material will be saved in the folder titled **In Model**.

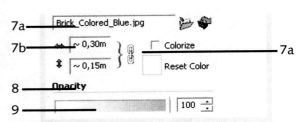

how to create a material from textures applied to coplanar faces

1. Select two or more faces (they should be on the same plane) with different textures (**a**). Right-click on either of the selected faces and select the **Combine Textures** option (**b**).

2. A window will open, asking if you want to delete the lines between the selected faces. Choose **Yes**.

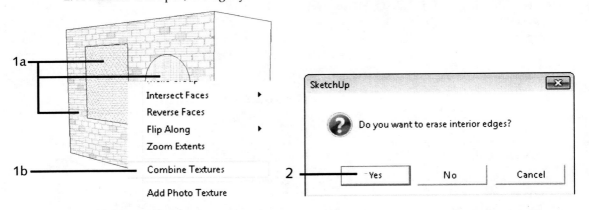

3. Choose **Window/Materials**, and notice that a new texture was created (**a**). By default, the name given the texture is **Material**, but you can give it any other name by typing it in the indicated field (**b**).

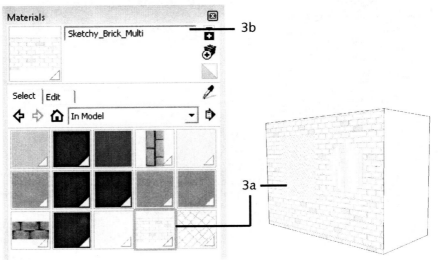

how to edit a material in another program

You can edit any material in a photo editor (such as Photoshop or Gimp, for example) from
SketchUp. After the changes has been made in the photo editor, it will automatically be updated
in your file.

1. Choose **Window/Preferences (a)** and click on **Applications (b)**.

2. Click on **Choose...** to select a default program for editing images.

3. Click **OK** to confirm the change.

4. Back on the drawing, right-click on the texture you want to edit and choose **Texture/Edit Texture
Image...**.

5. SketchUp will open the indicated program. Make the changes to the image and save without
changing the name.

6. Close the photo editor and go back on SketchUp; notice that the material was directly altered in
your project.

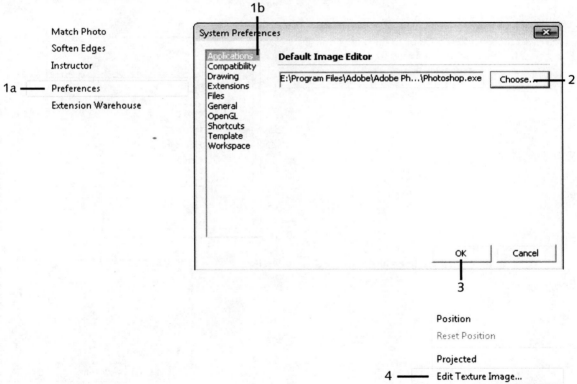

how to create a library

1. Choose **Window/ Materials.**

2. Click on the indicated tab and choose **Open or create a collection....**

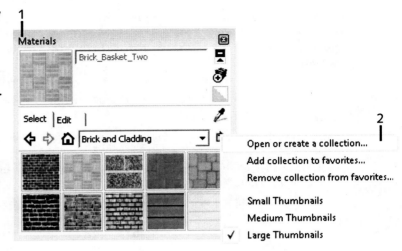

3. Choose a folder (**a**) or make a new one (**b**); In this case, make a new folder, type the name, then click **OK** (**c**).

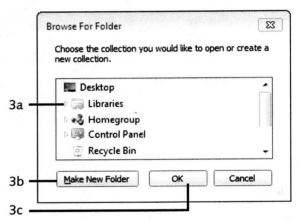

4. Your new library will be add into the dropdown list.

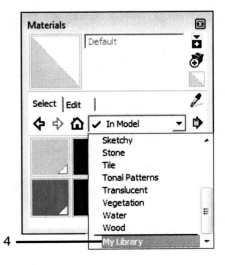

how to copy a material from one library to another

1. Choose **Window/Materials**.

2. Click the indicated button to open the secondary pane.

3. Click to select the library that contains your texture from the dropdown list.

4. On this other list, click to indicate the library to receive your texture.

5. Click on the texture you want to include and drag it to the lower window. Release it for SketchUp to copy the texture to the desired library.

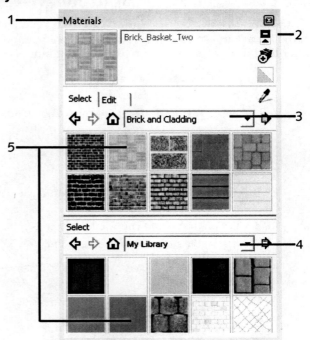

3.4 Colors and materials (textures) – Mac version

In addition to painting with solid colors, you can use SketchUp's vast materials library (textures). If the library doesn't have the image you want, choose from any on your computer. You can also alter the base image, adding a color or changing its opacity.

to apply a material to an object

1. Choose **Window/Materials**.

2. Choose **Texture Pallete** at the top of the window.

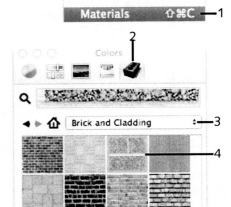

3. Select the library containing the texture you want from the drop list.

4. Click on the texture you want to use to paint.

5. Click on the surface you want to paint.

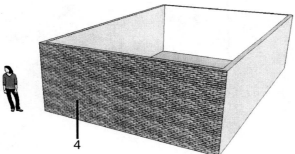

how to edit a material being used in a model

1. Choose **Window/Materials**.

2. Click on the indicated button to show all the material applied in the model.

3. Right-click on the material and choose **Edit....**

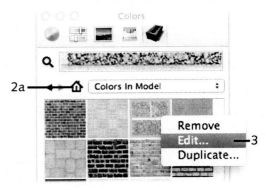

4. On the top of the window, choose the color system and find that you want to use for mixing the texture.

5. Enter the width and/or height (**a**) for the texture size. Click on the chain (**b**) to enable or disable proportional relation between the width and height of the texture.

6. If you'd like, alter the opacity of the material, by using the **Opacity** control.

7. Click on **Close** to finish the changes.

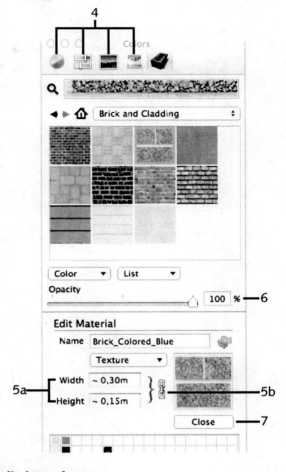

how to create a material from a texture applied to a face

1. Right-click on the texture to be copied and choose **Make Unique Texture**.

2. Choose **Window/Materials** and notice that a new texture has been created. The name of the texture is the same as before with an "_" added in the beginning and in the end.

how to create a new material

1. Choose **Window/Materials**.

2. Click on the indicated tab and choose **New Texture...**

3. Find the file texture (JPG, BMP, TIFF, etc.) previously saved in your computer (**a**), then click **Open** (**b**).

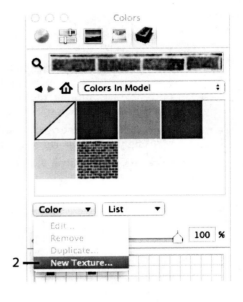

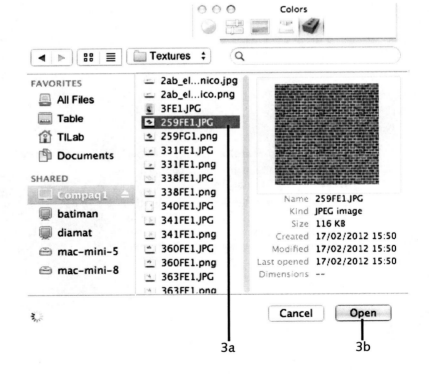

4. Type the material name and enter the desired width and/or height (**a**) for the texture size. Click the chain (**b**) to lock or unlock the aspect ratio of the texture. Then click **OK** (**c**).

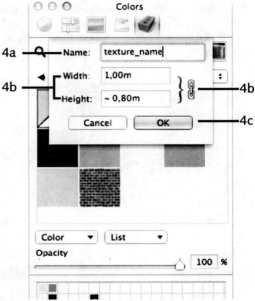

5. Right-click on the new texture and choose **Edit....** to make other modifications.

6. Use the color system on the top of the window to make changes in the texture color.

7. You also can change the **Opacity** to make a translucent material.

8. Click on **Close** to finish.

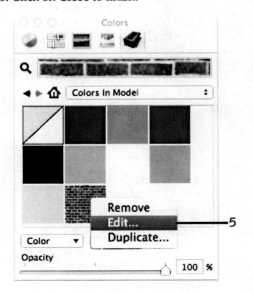

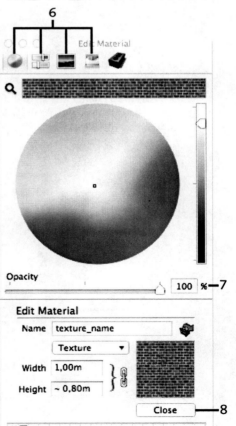

how to create a material from textures applied to coplanar faces

1. Select two or more faces (they should be on the same plane) with different textures (**a**). Right-click on either of the selected faces and select the **Combine Textures** option (**b**).

2. A window will open, asking if you want to delete the lines between the selected faces. Choose **Yes**.

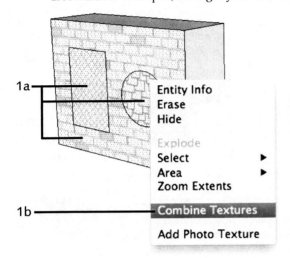

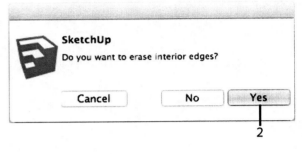

3. Choose **Window/Materials**. Click on **Colors in model** (**a**) and notice that a new texture was created (**b**). By default, the name given the texture is **Material**.

4. If you want to change the name, right-click on the created texture and choose **Edit....** Type the new name in the indicated field.

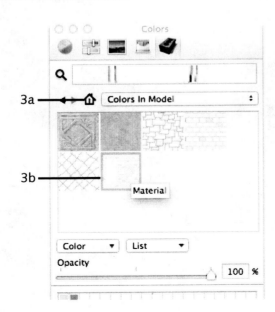

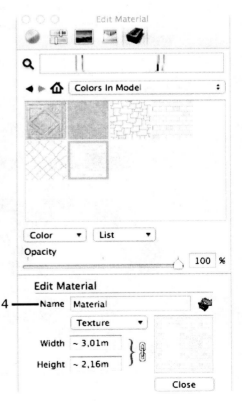

how to edit a material in another program

You can edit any material in a photo editor (such as Photoshop or Gimp, for example) from SketchUp. After the changes has been made in the photo editor, it will automatically be updated in your file.

1. Choose **SketchUp/Preferences...** (**a**) and click on **Applications** (**b**).

2. Click on **Choose...** to select a default program for editing images.

3. Close the window to confirm the change.

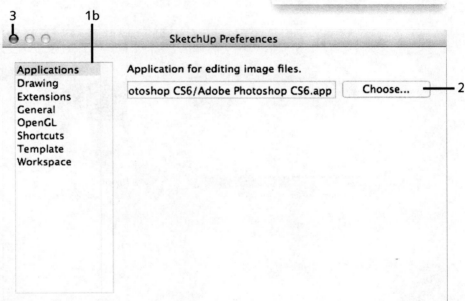

4. Back on the drawing, right-click on the texture you want to edit and choose **Texture/Edit Texture Image...**.

5. SketchUp will open the indicated program. Make the changes to the image and save without changing the name.

6. Close the photo editor and go back on SketchUp; notice that the material was directly altered in your project.

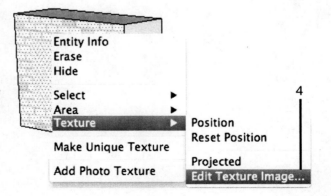

how to create a library

1. Choose **Window/Materials**.

2. Click on the indicated tab and choose **New....**

3. Type the name for your new library, then click **OK**.

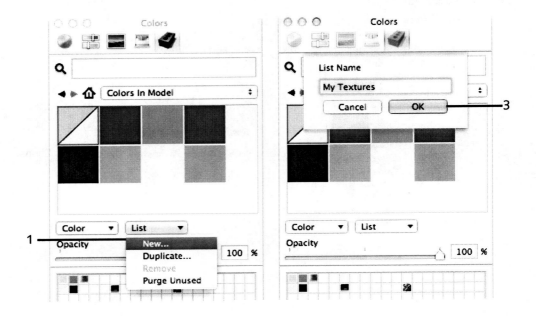

how to copy a material from one library to another

1. Choose **Window/Materials**.

2. Drag and drop the material to the favorites panel.

3. At the indicated tab choose the library that will receive your material.

4. Drag and drop the material into the list.

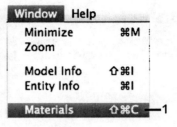

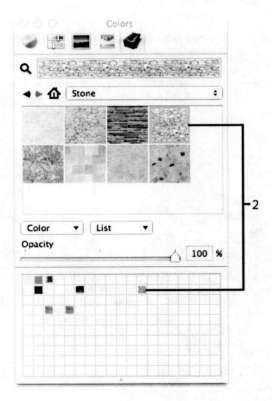

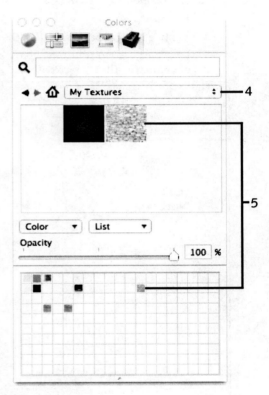

3.5 How to create objects with the aid of an image

One of the coolest characteristics of SketchUp is its ability to draw over imported images on a face. With this, you can use an actual picture as a reference for creating figures, and at the same time it serves as a texture.

to import an image and paint it on an object

1. Choose **File/Import....** Next, select the image file (JPG, BMP, TIF, etc.) you want.

2. In this same box, click the **Use as texture** button in the lower right.

3. Click on **Open**.

4. The image will appear, pinned to the cursor. Click on the face where you want to insert the image.

5. Move the cursor to adjust the image size. When sized correctly, click to confirm. SketchUp automatically fills the face with the image, repeating when necessary.

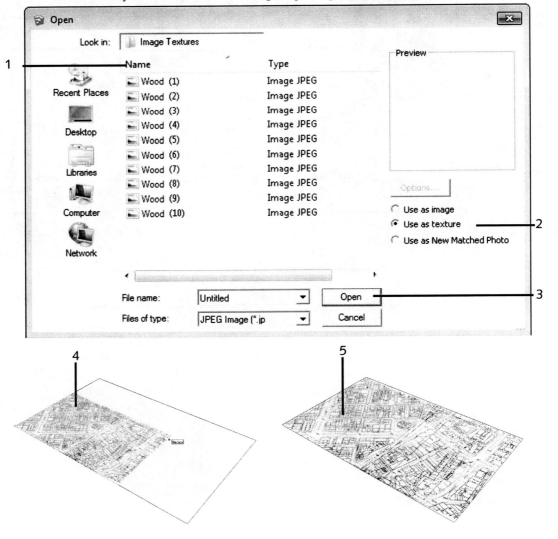

how to edit the applied image

1. Right-click on the image and choose **Texture/Position**.

2. Adjust the image, clicking and moving the controls described below:

    a. **Move**: Move the image by the face;

    b. **Scale/Rotate** (*green*): Alter and rotate the image;

    c. **Distort** (*yellow*): Distort the image;

    d. **Scale/Shear** (*blue*): Scale the image and give a parallelogram effect.

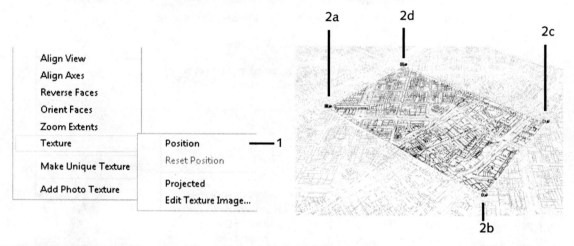

NOTE 1 Sometimes it's best to alter the image using four types of the **Distort** (*yellow*) control. To do this, right-click the image and choose **Fixed Pins**.

NOTE 2 To return the image to its original format, right-click it and choose **Texture/Reset Position**.

how to draw on an image

1. To draw on an image, just use the common drawing tools. Don't forget to draw the new lines on the face, watching for the **On Face** hint (blue block). After making a few lines over the face containing the image, use the **Push/Pull** tool to change the volume of the object.

2. In as many new figures you create from the photo, the new faces will appear to be painted with pieces of the original image, giving it a slightly strange appearance. You can paint them using colors and materials, as seen in section **3.3 Colors and materials (textures)**, on page **89**.

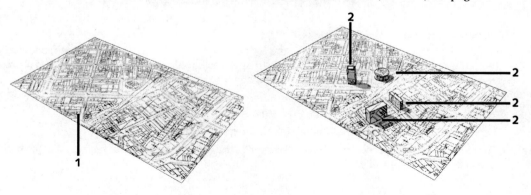

3.6 How to create objects with Match Photo

The group of tools called **Match Photo** makes it possible to create a 3D model from one or more pictures taken of a real site or a perspective drawing. This resource also enables the photo insertion of a project.

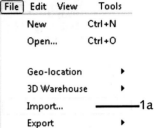

to import an image to be used with Match Photo

1. Choose **File/Import...** (**a**). Next, select the image file (JPG, BMP, TIF, etc.) you want to use (**b**).

2. In this same box, click on **Use as New Matched Photo**, in the lower right.

3. Click on **Open**.

4. The image will appear in the screen background; next, you will adjust the viewer so that the vanishing points are relative to the image.

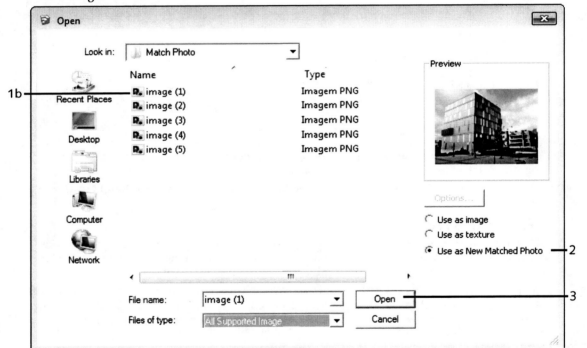

how to adjust the vanishing points

To adjust the vanishing points, make it so the four colored, lateral lines (red and green) are aligned with the object that is the main focus of the image. You should also move the point that represents the intersection of the three axes to the area where the project will be drawn.

1. Adjust the first red dashed line using the side controls and/or by the line itself, until you're able to adjust it in a way by which it is aligned with a strip of the image.

2. Do the same with the other red line and with the green lines as well.

3. Position the point representing the axes' center in the area of the image to be the start point of the project.

4. In the **Match Photo** window, click on **Done** to finish.

5. SketchUp returns to the template. If you want to make another adjustment to the vanishing points, click the indicated button, in the **Match Photo** window.

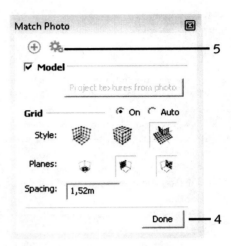

> **NOTE** An image imported as a matched photo is automatically saved in a scene. Every time you change your position in the program, the image will disappear, only to return when you activate the scene containing the matched photo.

other interesting options

1. To draw on an image, just use the common drawing tools. Don't forget to draw the new lines on the face, watching for the **On Face** hint (blue block). After making a few lines over the face containing the image, use the **Push/Pull** tool to change the volume of the object.

2. You can use the image itself to paint the faces you created. This method allows you to create new objects using your picture as a reference, since SketchUp can reconstruct the object image as if the picture was taken in front of it. To do this, select all the objects that will absorb the image, right-click and choose **Project Photo**.

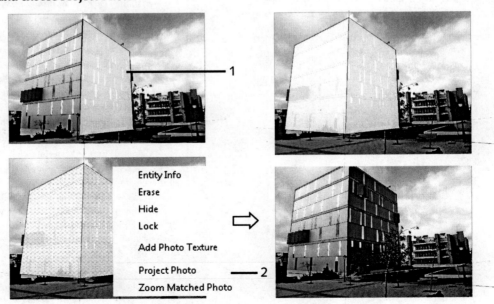

Chapter highlights

Display (p. 80)

On the **Face Style** menu, choose from among the display options: **Wireframe, Hidden Line, Shaded, Shaded with Textures,** or **Monochrome**.

X-Ray mode adds a transparent effect to the display styles listed above. To use it, Choose **Face Styles** menu and click the **X-Ray** button.

Configure shadows (p. 82)

Choose **Window/Shadows** and click the **Display/Hide Shadows** box.

Set the **Time** by using the bar or by typing it in the side field, and select the **Date**.

In **Light**, adjust the amount of light that is applied directly on the faces of the objects; on the **Dark** bar, adjust the intensity of the shadows projected.

Match Photo (p. 106)

The group of tools called **Match Photo** makes it possible to create a 3D project from one or more pictures taken of a real project or a perspective drawing. This resource also enables the photo insert of a project.

Styles (p. 83)

SketchUp allows many other changes to the display settings of your project. Changes to line styles, display of faces, sky and ground settings can be made. It's also possible to insert watermarks and configure the face and line styles for SketchUp tools.

You can make all these adjustments and save them as a **Style**. You can create various styles, or just use those that come with the program.

Colors and materials (textures)

How to apply a material to an object (p. 89)

On the **Principal** toolbar, choose **Paint Bucket**. The **Materials** window will open. Click on **Select** to select one of the texture libraries. Select the library that contains the texture you want; click on the texture you want to use to paint; click on the face you want to paint.

How to edit an existing material (p. 89)

Choose **Window/Materials**; in **Select** field, choose the library that contains the material you want; select the material, then click the **Edit** button; on the color palette, find the color you want to use for mixing the texture.

How to create a new material (p. 91)

Choose **Window/Materials** and click on **Create Material**. If you want to use an image as the base of the material, click on **Use Texture**, then click on the folder icon; choose an image file and click **OK**. On the color palette, find the color you want to use for mixing the texture; click the **Add** button to save the active material.

To include a material in a library (p. 95)

Choose **Window/Materials**; click the button to open the secondary pane. In the first window, select the library with your file and find your texture. Don't click yet. In the second window select the library that will be receiving your texture; click and drag your texture from the first window to the second.

Suggested activities

Ex. 01 – Styles

1. Open the **Cap03_Ex01.skp** file.

2. Configure the styles according to the following:

    a. **Edge**: Activate the **Display Edges**, **Profiles**, **Depth Cue**, **Extension**, **Endpoints**, and **Jitter** options. Change the color of the dash, using the button beside **Color** (*fig. 25*);

    b. **Face**: Select the **Shaded with Textures** button, don't activate the **X-Ray** button, activate the **Enable Transparency** box and place the **Transparency Quality** on **Faster**;

    c. **Background**: Activate the **Sky** and **Ground** options, and change their colors in the corresponding boxes. Keep the **Transparency** control on medium (*fig. 26*);

    d. **Watermark**: Insert the **SketchUpPro_stepbystep.png** file as a watermark. Enable the **Blend** option; drag the bar to the right. Place the image in the lower left corner (*fig. 27*);

    e. **Modeling**: Alter only the color of the **Section Cuts**.

3. Save the style under the name **SketchUp Book Style**.

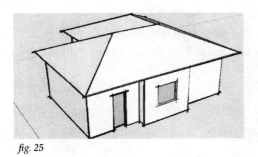

fig. 25

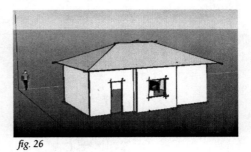

fig. 26

fig. 27

Ex. 02 – Textures

1. Open the **Cap03_Ex02.skp** file and apply textures to all the elements (*fig. 28*):

    a. Apply a texture from the **Vegetation** options to the grass;

    b. Apply **Asphalt** and **Concrete** textures to the floors of the house and pool;

    c. Use a **Water** texture for the water in the pool;

    d. For the interior walls, use a texture from the list in the **Colors**;

    e. For the exterior walls, import an image, for example, the imaged filed under the name *Brick_Rough_Tan.jpg* in the exercises' folder;

    f. For the floor, import the *Wood_Floor_Light.jpg* image.

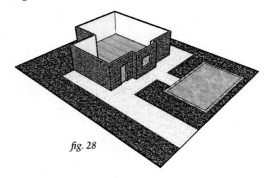

fig. 28

Ex. 03 – Modeling from a picture

1. Open the **Cap03_Ex03.skp** file.

2. Import the *Elevation.jpg* image as a texture and place it on largest side (*fig. 29*).

3. Make rectangles and polygons based on the image and then use the **Push/Pull** tool to alter the volume of the frontage (*figs. 30* and *31*).

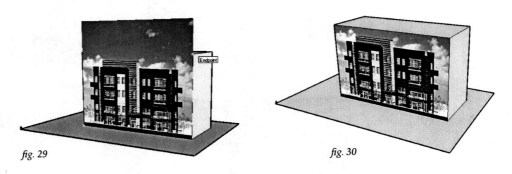

fig. 29   *fig. 30*

fig. 31

Ex. 04 – Modeling with Match Photo

1. Open the **Cap03_Ex04.skp** file.

2. Import the image *Perspective.jpg* as a matched photo.

3. Place the point of reference on the corner of the building and adjust the colored axes (*fig. 32*).

4. Use the **Line** and **Rectangle** tools to draw the main body of the building (*fig. 33*).

5. Select the faces created over the image and use the **Project Photo** command (*fig. 34*).

6. Move the position of the viewer to see the result. Draw new polygons and rectangles, and use the **Push/Pull** tool to alter the volume of the building (*fig. 35*).

fig. 32

fig. 33

fig. 34

fig. 35

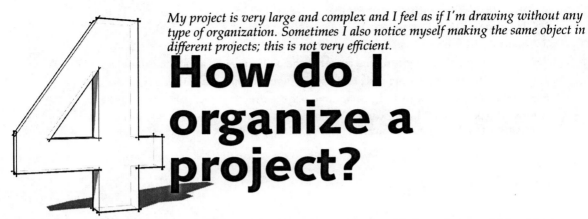

My project is very large and complex and I feel as if I'm drawing without any type of organization. Sometimes I also notice myself making the same object in different projects; this is not very efficient.

How do I organize a project?

Organizing a project is fundamental in various aspects: whether it's it to show or hide objects with common characteristics or creating groups of objects that can easily be identified, stored, and utilized in any project. SketchUp offers these organizational possibilities, explained in the following.

What you'll read in this chapter

4.1 Groups

4.2 Components

4.3 Dynamic components

4.4 Outliner

4.5 Layers

4.1 Groups

SketchUp allows you to select various objects and transform them into a group. By doing this, it's possible to move, duplicate, and delete a group of objects in just one motion. It's possible and perfectly normal to have groups inside another one. You can always move objects (and groups, of course) inside and outside the groups you've made. There is also a command, called **Explode**, used to ungroup your objects when it's necessary.

howe to create a group

1. Select one or more objects.

2. Choose **Edit/Create Group** (or right-click on one of the objects and choose **Make Group**).

3. To name the group, select it in the drawing area, and in the **Entity Info** window (**a**), enter a **Name** (**b**). Each group can have a different name.

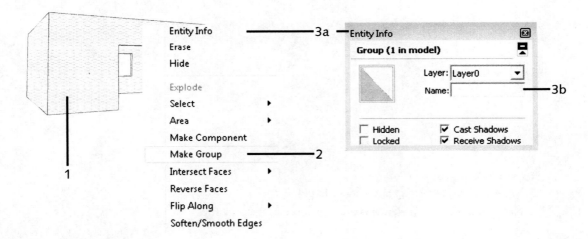

how to edit a group

1. Double-click on the group you want to edit, or right-click and choose **Edit Group**.

2. Notice that at the moment, the rest of the drawing appears in a grey tone, and the group is highlighted.

3. Use the normal drawing tools.

4. To exit the group, choose **Edit/Close Group/Component**, or click on an empty area of the drawing.

to explode a group

1. Right-click on the group and choose **Explode**.

2. Notice that the group elements are now loose in the drawing.

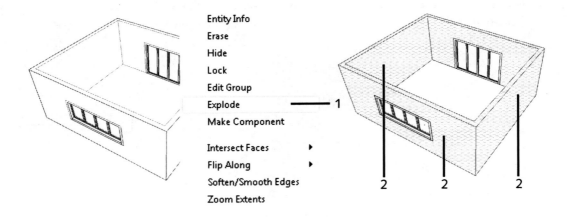

4.2 Components

Component is the name given to an entity, a special type of group, that can contain one or more objects. In opposite of a common group, a component remains available in a library to be used several times in the same file or be sent to another file. When we modify the drawing of a component in a file, all the identical components will be automatically modify. These and other important properties are explained below.

how to create a component

1. Select one or more objects.

2. Choose **Edit/Make Component** (or right-click on the objects and select **Make Component**).

3. Configure the items in the box:

   a. The **Name** of the component;

   b. On **Glue To**, select the kind of face that this component will align to. Then, you can use the **Cut opening** option to indicate if the object is to cut a face, if it's touching one (you can use this for components representing doors or windows);

   c. In the field **Always face camera**, make it so the component is always facing front towards the the viewer. This is very useful when the component represents trees, people, etc.;

   d. The box **Replace selection with component** works in a way that upon closing the window, the original drawing is substituted by the recently created component.

4. To finish, click on **Create**.

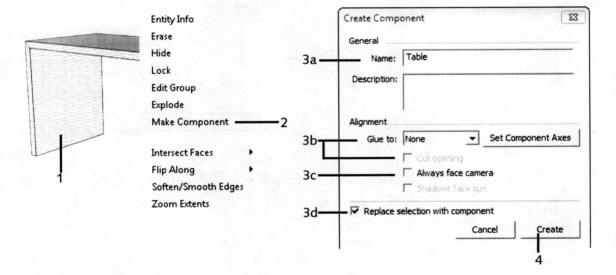

5. Notice the component created appears on the **Window/Components** menu option, called **In Model**.

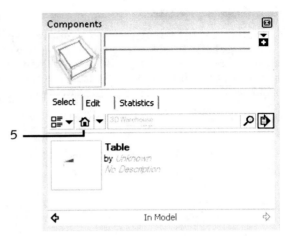

NOTE To create components that make openings in walls, like doors and windows, it's necessary to draw them as in a floor plan (lying) for the **Glue to** tool to work (item **3b**).

how to insert a component

1. Choose **Window/Components**.

Model Info

Entity Info

Materials

1 ——— Components

Styles

Layers

Outliner

2. Click the indicated button (**a**), then select the folder containing (or that may contain) the component you want (**b**).

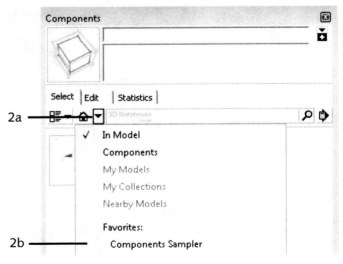

3. If the component you want doesn't appear in any folder, you can search for it by typing a text in the indicated field. Upon pressing **Enter**, SketchUp will connect to the 3D Warehouse to attempt to find the component (you will need an active internet connection for this).

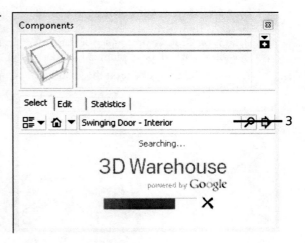

4. Choose the component by clicking on it, then clicking where you want to insert it. If you prefer, click and move the component directly to the drawing, releasing the cursor in the desired location.

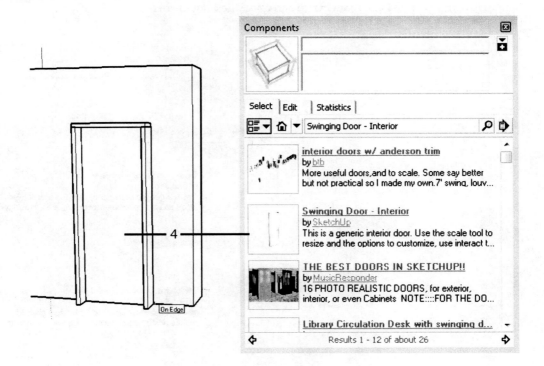

how to insert a component in a wall

To correctly insert the component into a wall, it's best to create it "lying on the floor" of your file, and the **Glue To** option should be on **Vertical**. There are many ways to insert a component into a wall. What will be explained ahead isn't the simplest way, but it is what works best in all cases.

1. Create the component on the ground plane, with the **Glue to** option on **Vertical**, as mentioned before.

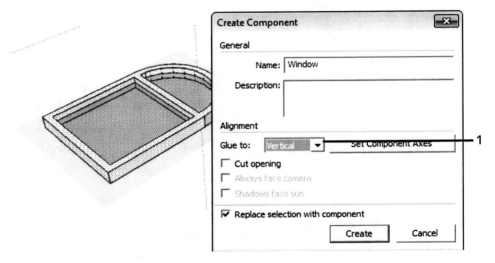

2. Choose **Window/Components** (**a**) and select the component (**b**).

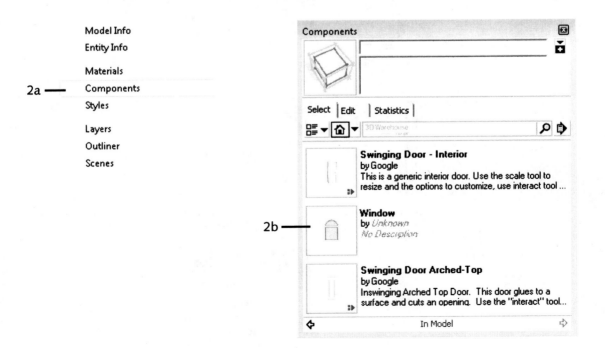

3. Insert it in the wall you want.

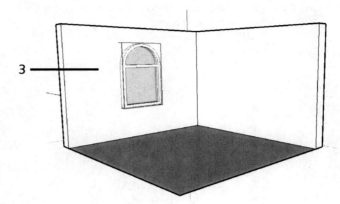

4. Select the component and the face of the wall, right-click and choose **Intersect Faces/ With Selection**.

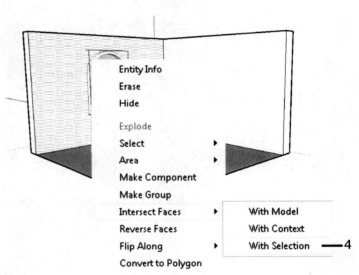

5. Right-click the component and choose **Hide**.
You'll notice the outline of the component is marked on the wall; depending on the component's design, some of the lines will be drawn inside the outline.

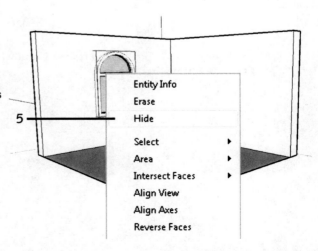

6. Delete the lines that may exist inside the outline using the **Select** and **Eraser** tools.

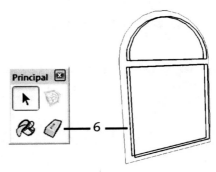

7. Click with the **Push/ Pull** tool (**a**) on the indicated face (**b**), then click and drag until you reach the border of the other face of the wall (**c**), to create the opening.

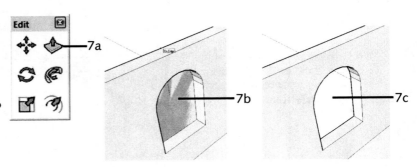

8. Choose **View/Hidden Geometry** to see the hidden component again.

9. Right-click on the component and choose **Unhide** (**a**). Notice that the component has returned to full view as normal (**b**).

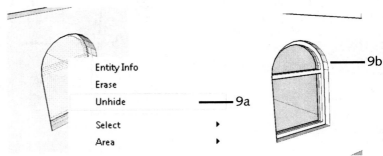

how to edit a component

1. Double-click the component you want to edit, or right-click and choose **Edit Component**.

2. Notice that at this moment, the rest of the drawing appears in a grey tone and the component is highlighted.

3. Use the normal drawing tools. Notice that all the copies of that same component, in the same file, are automatically altered.

4. To exit the component, choose **Edit/Close Group/Component**, or click on an empty area of the drawing.

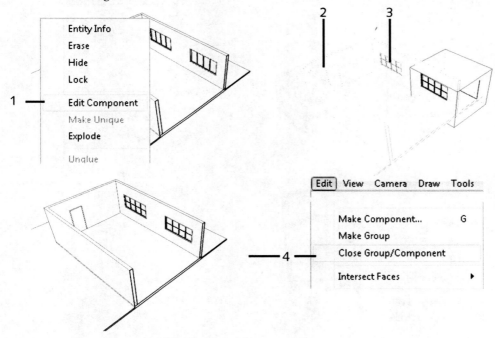

to create a component from another

Suppose you have a chair with a support for notebooks and you need one without the support. To avoid having to create the component from scratch, try the following:

1. If you only have one component in the drawing, insert another.

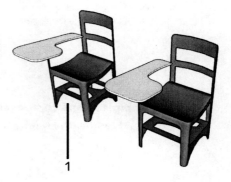

2. Right-click on one of the components and choose **Make Unique**.

3. SketchUp automatically creates a new component. Choose **Window/Components** and notice the newly created component, by clicking on the **In Model** bar.

4. To rename the component, select it in the drawing area, choose**Window/Entity Info** and type it in the **Definition Name** field. Notice that all the copies of this component were renamed as well.

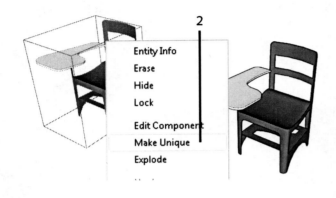

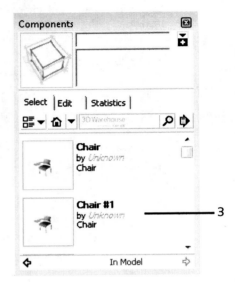

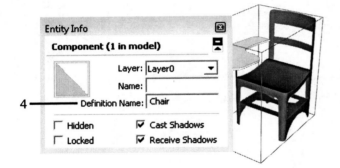

5. To edit the new component, double-click on it and make the alterations (in this case, remove the support).

how to replace one component with another

1. Choose **Window/Components**.

Model Info

Entity Info

Materials

1— Components

Styles

2. Right-click on the component you wish to replace.

3. Click on **Reload**.

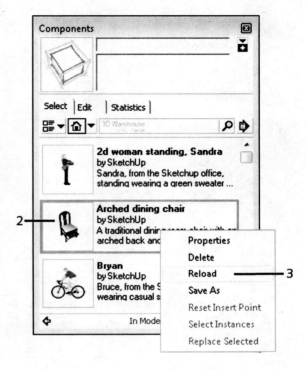

4. You will be asked whether you want to substitute the component. Choose **Yes**.

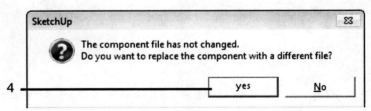

5. Find the new component.

6. Click on **Open**.

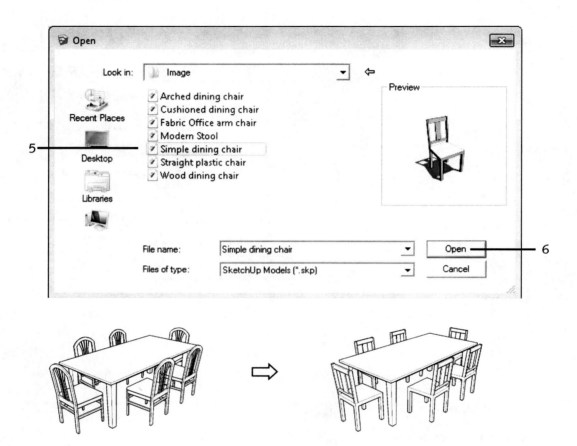

how to create a library

1. Choose **Window/Components**.

2. Click on the indicated arrow (**a**), then click on **Open or create a local collection... (b)**.

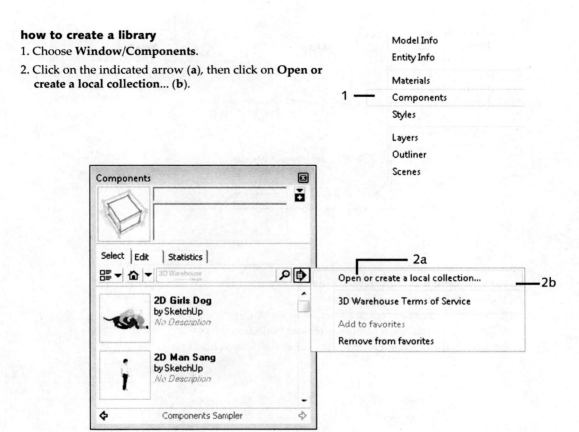

3. Next, click on the indicated button to create a new folder (**a**), then name it. Press **Enter** to confirm. Click on **OK** (**b**) to close the window.

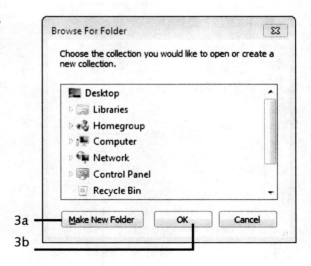

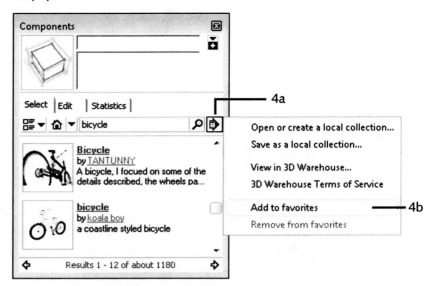

4. After creating the folder, you can add it to the favorites list. To do this, click on the indicated button (**a**), then click on **Add to favorites** (**b**).

How to save a component to the library

1. Choose **Window/Components**.
2. Find the component you'll be saving to the library.
3. Click on the indicated button (secondary selection pane).
4. Click on the indicated arrow (**a**) to select the desired library (**b**).

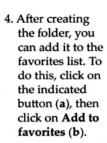

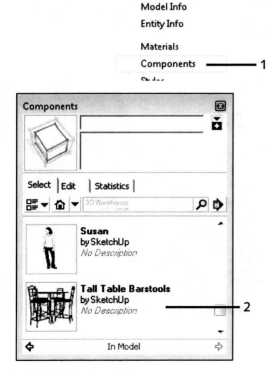

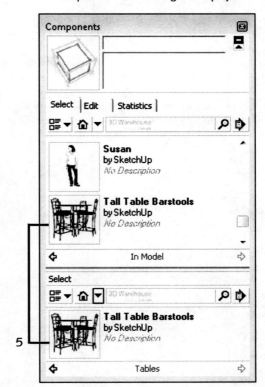

5. Click and drag the component to the library.

to save a 3D Warehouse search as a local library

You can save objects that are the result of a search. This is a good way to keep the ones you use frequently, without the need to connect to the internet every time. To do this:

1. Choose **Window/Components**.

2. Search in the indicated field and press **Enter** (**a**). The search result will appear in the window below briefly after (**b**).

3. Click on the indicated arrow (**a**), then click on **Save as a local collection...** (**b**).

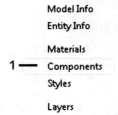

Model Info

Entity Info

Materials

1 — Components

Styles

Layers

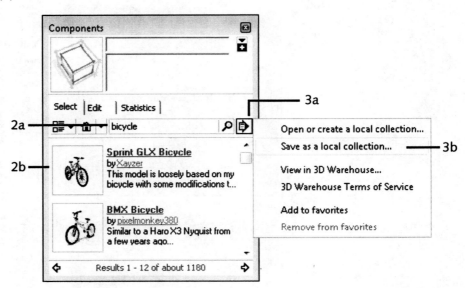

4. In the box, choose a folder to store the objects (**a**) or create a new one (**b**). After, click on **OK** to confirm (**c**).

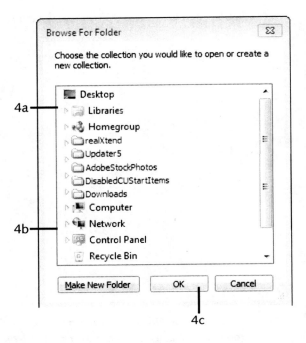

5. After downloading the objects, you can add the folder to the favorites list. To do this, click on the indicated button (**a**), then click on **Add to favorites** (**b**).

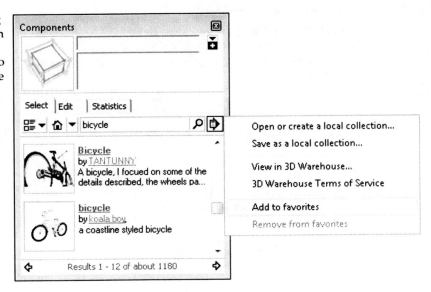

4.3 Dynamic components

A dynamic component is a special type of object. Using the **Component Options** window, you can alter various parameters of the component (height, width, length, color, among others) without having to redraw the object. Some dynamic components have special attributes: change the size without scaling the internal elements, alternate internal pieces, or even move parts using the **Interact** tool. A dynamic component can be identified, in the **Components** window, by a green mark beside each drawing, as you can see in the image on the side.

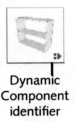

Dynamic
Component
identifier

how to alter dynamic component measurements

1. Choose **Window/Components** (**a**). For this example, you will click on the indicated button (**b**) and select **Dynamic Components Training** (**c**).

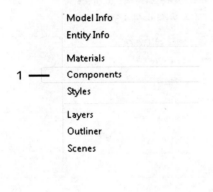

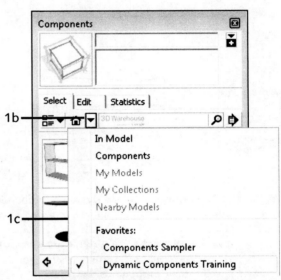

2. Choose **Basic Shelving Unit** and insert it into the drawing.

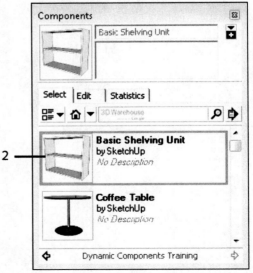

3. With the component selected, choose **Window/Component Options**. Configure the items in the box:

   a. Object color, in **Material**;
   b. The **Depth**, the **Height** and the **Width** of the object;
   c. The **Thickness** of the pieces.

4. To finish, click on **Apply** and notice that the component was altered in the drawing.

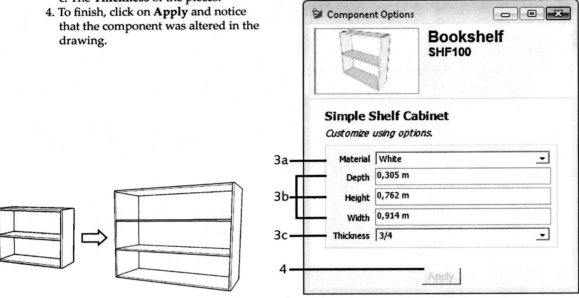

NOTE Every time you alter a dynamic component, SketchUp creates a new component in your file, adding **#1**, or **#2** to the name, according to each case.

how to interact with a dynamic component

1. Choose **Window/Components (a)**. For this example, you will click on the indicated button (b) to select the **Components Sampler (c)**.

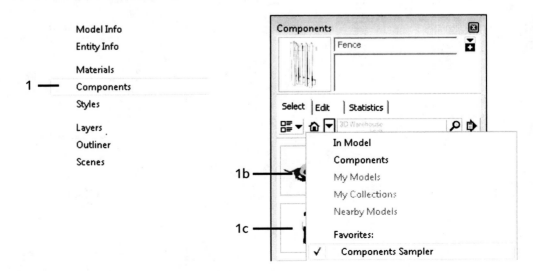

2. Select the component **Archtop Door** and insert it into a vertical face of the drawing.

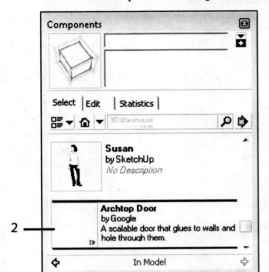

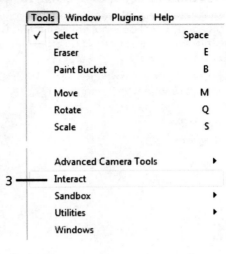

3. Choose **Tools/Interact** (**a**), then click on the door you just inserted (**b**). Notice the door opening. Click once more (**c**) to close the door again.

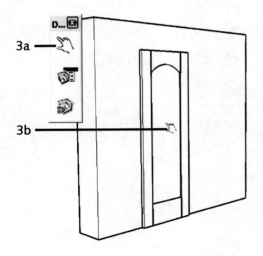

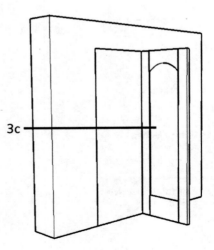

the relationship between dynamic components and scale

When you use the **Scale** tool on certain dynamic components, they are altered in a particular manner. The tool does not scale all internal elements proportionally as it would be expected, but redraws the entire object adding more elements if necessary (more steps on stairs, for example). Try this example:

1. Choose **Window/Components** (**a**). For this example, you will click the indicated button (**b**) to select the **Components Sampler** (**c**).

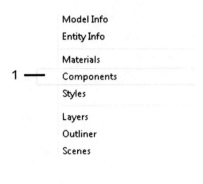

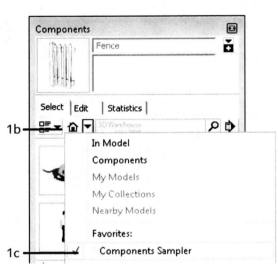

2. Select the **Stairs Floating** component and insert it into the drawing.

3. On the **Edit toolbars**, choose the **Scale** tool.

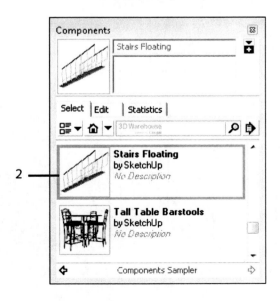

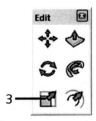

4. Various control points will appear. Click on one of the control points at the base or top of the stairs (**a** or **b**) and move the cursor to resize the stairs.

5. Click to confirm. Notice that in just a few seconds, the stairs are redrawn and steps are added or removed, according to the motion done as in **4**.

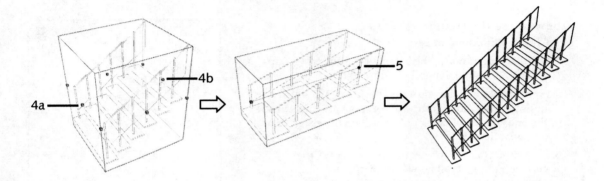

4.4 Outliner

The **Outliner** window offers a quick and practical way to view and have access to objects that are organized in groups or components. This panel is especially useful when the project is complex, as it allows for instantly selecting objects which are inside components that may be inside of others, respectively. It also allows for reorganization of component hierarchy (place an object inside another).

how to use the Outliner window

1. Choose **Window/Outliner**.

2. In the window, notice the list of all the objects (groups and components) that exist in the project.

3. Some names may have a **+** sign beside them, which indicates that more groups or components exists inside the one you are viewing now. Click on the **+** sign to find out what there is.

4. Each time you click on a name in the list (**a**), the corresponding object is selected in the drawing window. To edit it, right-click on the name and select the **Edit Group** or **Edit Component** option (**b**), or instead, you can right-click on the object itself, in the drawing window (**c**).

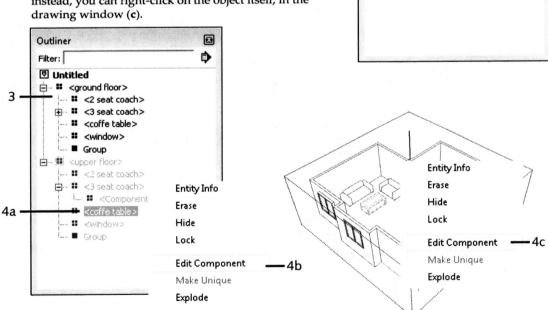

4.5 Layers

You can use the SketchUp layers system to classify the different types of drawings that exist in a project. For example, a residential project can have layers for roofing, walls, furniture, floors, landscaping, etc. This separation is very useful when you need to hide a category of the drawing without creating another file and deleting objects.

to create a layer

1. Choose **Window/Layers**.

2. Click on the **Add** button and notice how SketchUp automatically creates and names the layer. At that time, you can rename the layer.

3. If you prefer, you can rename the layer later, by double-clicking it.

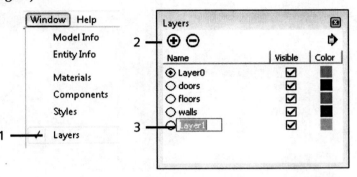

how to use color in a layer

You can associate a color with a layer and have the option of painting all the objects included in the layer with this color. To set a layer color:

1. Choose **Window/Layers** and click on the small block beside the name of the desired layer.

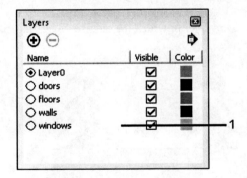

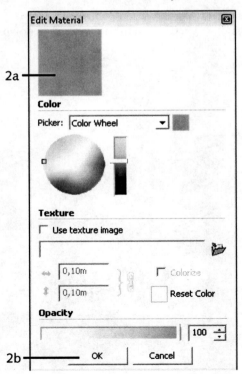

2. Next, choose the color you want (**a**) and click **OK** (**b**).

3. To make so all layers color objects, click
the button in the upper right of the **Layers**
window (**a**) and choose **Color by layer** (**b**).

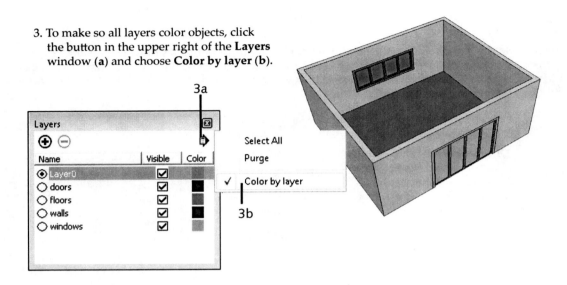

how to place an object from the drawing in a layer

1. Select the desired object.

2. Choose **Window/Entity Info**.

3. Click on the indicated dropdown list to choose the layer in which the object will be placed.

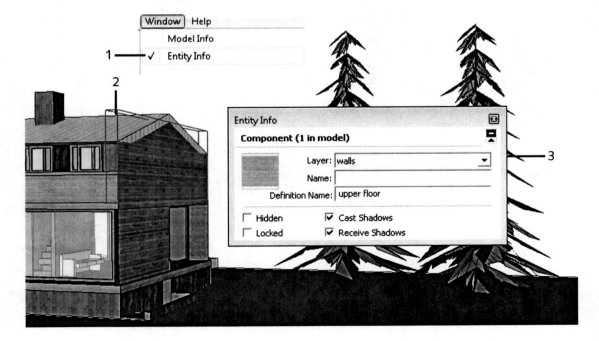

other layer operations

1. To show or hide a layer, click the **Visible** box, beside the name of the corresponding layer.

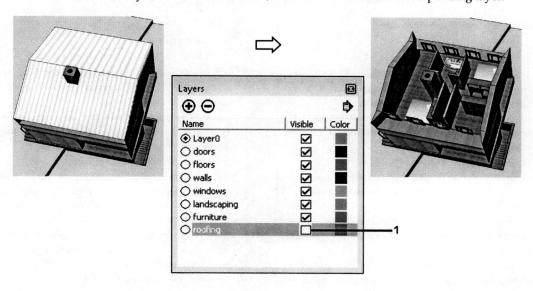

2. To delete a layer, select it from the list and click on the indicated button.

3. If the layer contains an object, you'll have the choose from **Move contents to Default layer, Move contents to Current layer**, or **Delete contents**.

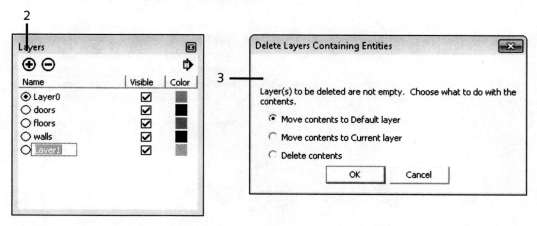

NOTE It's not possible to delete **Layer0**.

Chapter highlights

Groups

How to create a group (p. 113)

Select one or more objects and choose **Edit/Make Group** menu (or right-click on the objects and select **Create Group**). To name the group, select it in the drawing area and in the **Entity Info** window, enter the name in the **Name** field. Each group can have a different name.

How to edit a group (p. 113)

Double-click on the group you want to edit or right-click and choose **Edit Group**; use the drawing tools as normal.

To exit the group, choose **Edit/Close Group/Component** menu, or click on an empty area of the drawing.

To explode a group (p. 114)

Right-click the group and choose **Explode**; notice that all the group elements are now loose in the drawing.

Components

How to create a component (p. 115)

Select one or more objects and choose **Edit/Create Component**. In the box that opens, enter a name for the component, in the **Name** field.

The **Replace Selection with Component** box works to, upon closing the window, substitute the original drawing with the recently created component.

How to insert a component (p. 116)

Choose **Window/Components** to select the folder containing the component you want. If the component you want does not appear in any folder, search for it by entering a text in the corresponding field.

Upon pressing **Enter**, SketchUp connects to the 3D Warehouse to search for the component (you will need an active internet connection for this).

Select the component by clicking on it, then click where you want to insert it.

How to edit a component (p. 121)

Double-click on the component and notice how the rest of the drawing appears in a grey tone and it is highlighted. Use the drawing tools as usual. To exit the edit screen, choose **Edit/Close Group/Component** menu, or click on an empty area of the drawing.

To save a component in the library (p. 126)

Choose **Window/Components** and find the component you want to save to the library. Click the **Display secondary selection pane** button; click and drag the component to the library.

Dynamic components

How to alter the dynamic component measurements (p. 129)

Choose **Window/Components** to select the dynamic component to be used; with the component selected, choose **Window/Component Options**. Next, configure items such as the color of the object, depth, height, width, among others that can be enabled for the selected object.

How to interact with a dynamic component (p. 130)

Choose **Window/Components**, to select the dynamic component to be used; choose **Tools/Interact** and then click on the interactive part of the object.

The relationship between dynamic components and scale (p. 132)

Choose **Window/Components** to select the dynamic component to be used. On the **Edit toolbar,** choose the **Scale** tool. Various control points will appear. Click on one of the points and move the cursor to resize the object. Click to confirm. Notice that in just a few seconds, the object is redrawn, with more or less internal components that continue to maintain their size.

Outliner (p. 134)

Choose **Window/Outliner**; notice in the window, the list of all the objects (groups and components) in your project. Some names may have a + sign beside them. This indicates that more groups and components exist inside the one you are viewing now. Click on the + sign to find out what they are. Each time you click on a name in the list, the corresponding objects is selected in the drawing window.

Layers (p. 135)

You can use the SketchUp layers system to classify the different types of drawing in the project.

For example, a residential project may have layers for roofing, walls, furniture, floors, landscaping, etc.

This separation is very useful when needing to hide all of a category in a drawing without the need to create a new file and delete objects.

To create a layer, choose **Window/Layers** and click the + button.

How to use color in a layer (p. 135)

Choose **Window/Layers** and click on the small block beside the desired layer; next, select the color you want and click **OK**. To make it so all the objects in a layer are colored, click on the button in the upper right of the **Layers** window and then choose the option **Color by Layer**.

How to place an object in a drawing in a layer (p. 136)

Select the desired object and choose **Window/Entity Info** to select the layer in which to place the object.

Suggested activities

Ex. 01 – Groups

1. Open the **Cap04_Ex01.skp** file.

2. Select the elements that make the bookshelf; next, use the **Edit/Make Group** menu (*fig. 36*).

3. With the **Move** tool, take the bookshelf into the house (*fig. 37*).

4. Use the **Move** tool to duplicate the object. Place it beside the first bookshelf (*fig. 38*).

5. Double-click on the group and alter the paint texture of the bookshelf (*fig. 39*). Notice that the alterations were only made to this bookshelf.

Edit	View	Camera	Window	Help

Undo Push/Pull   Alt+Backspace

Redo   Ctrl+Y

Cut   Shift+Delete

Copy   Ctrl+C

Make Component..   G

Make Group

fig. 36

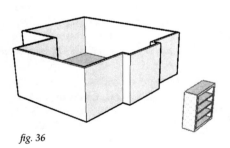

fig. 36

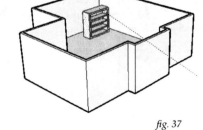

fig. 37

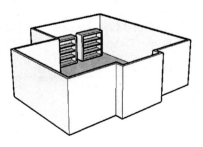

fig. 38

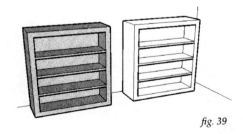

fig. 39

Ex. 02 – Components

1. Open the **Cap04_Ex02.skp** file.
2. Select the elements of the table. Right-click on them and use the **Make Component** command (*fig. 40*). Name the component and click on **Create**.
3. Choose **Window/Components** and click the **In Model** button. Notice that your component is saved there.
4. Place the table in the house with the **Move** tool.
5. Create four copies of the table, again using the **Move** tool (*fig. 41*).
6. Double-click on either of the tables, change a texture applied to it. Notice that the alterations are automatically reproduced on the other tables. Click on an empty area of the screen to exit the component edit.
7. Select two tables, right-click on one of them and choose the **Make Unique** option.
8. Double-click on one of these two tables and make an alteration to the component. Notice that this time the alteration was only repeated on the table that received the **Make Unique** command, given in step number **7** (*fig. 42*).

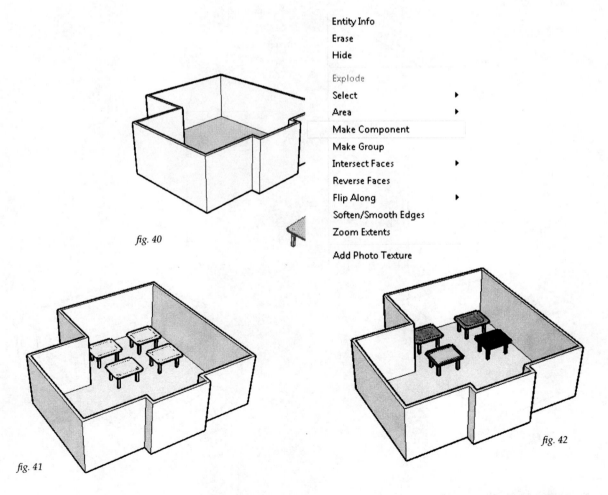

fig. 40

fig. 41

fig. 42

Ex. 03 – Component in wall

1. Open the **Cap04_Ex03.skp** file.
2. Select all the elements that make up the window and create the component (*fig. 43*). Don't forget to activate the **Glue to Vertical** option.
3. Choose **Window/Components** and click on the **In Model** button (*fig. 44*). Click and drag your window to a wall of the house.
4. Complete the procedures to make the wall opening; peel the window from the wall with the **Unglue** tool and place it, aligned with the internal face (*fig. 45*).

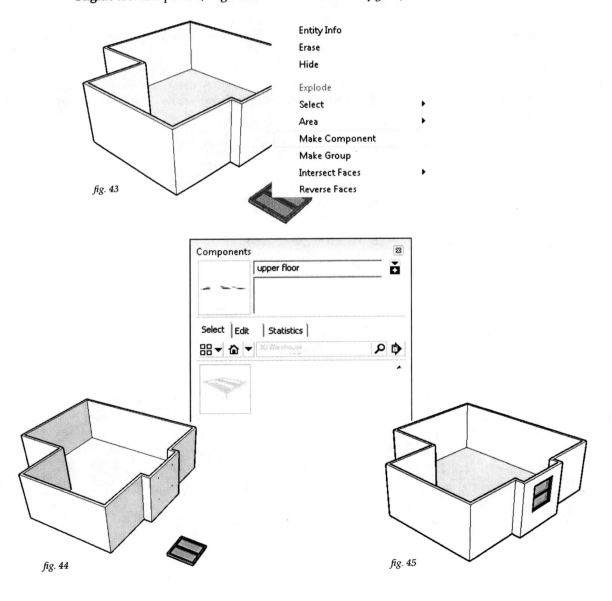

fig. 43

fig. 44

fig. 45

Ex. 04 – Dynamic component

1. Open the **Cap04_Ex04.skp** file.

2. Choose **Window/Components** and click on the **Components Sampler** folder.

3. Insert the **Bed** component in the drawing; use the **Component Options** window to change the type of bed to **CA King** (*fig. 46*).

4. Insert the **Couch** component; use the **Scale** tool to change the size of the couch (use the scale factor 1.2); use the **Component Options** window to change the size of the pillows to 20" or 0,5 m (*fig. 46*).

5. Insert the **Stairs Floating** component; use the **Scale** tool to change the size of the stairs; use the **Component Options** window to change the dimensions in relation to the mirror and the base of each step (*fig. 46*).

6. Insert the **Car Sedan** component; use the **Interact** tool to open and close the doors, move the front tires, and change the color of the car (*fig. 46*).

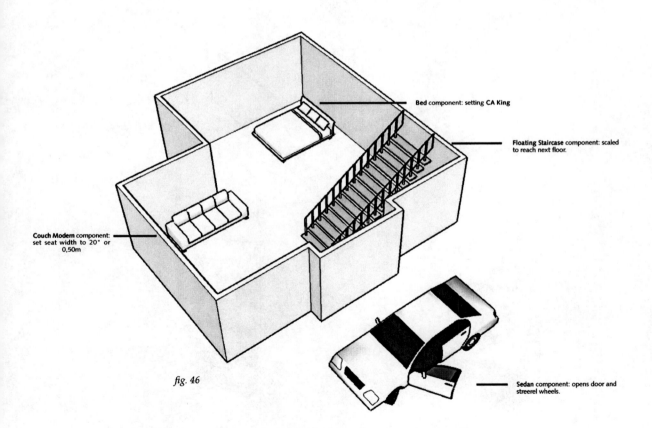

Bed component: setting **CA King**

Floating Staircase component: scaled to reach next floor.

Couch Modern component: set seat width to 20" or 0,50m

fig. 46

Sedan component: opens door and streerel wheels.

Ex. 05 – Outliner

1. Open the file **Cap04_Ex05.skp**.

2. Choose **Window/Outliner** and see how the components helped on the project organization (*fig. 47*).

3. Locate the **Shelf** component, inside the **Ground Floor**.

4. Double-click the **Shelf** and make any change to it. Notice that this same change was made to the other shelf, which is at the **Upper Floor** (*figs. 48a* and *48b*).

5. Still at the **Outliner** window, click on the other components to know better how a project can be organized. Notice, for example, the book components inside the **Shelf**, or still, how the **Two-seater Couch** component was created.

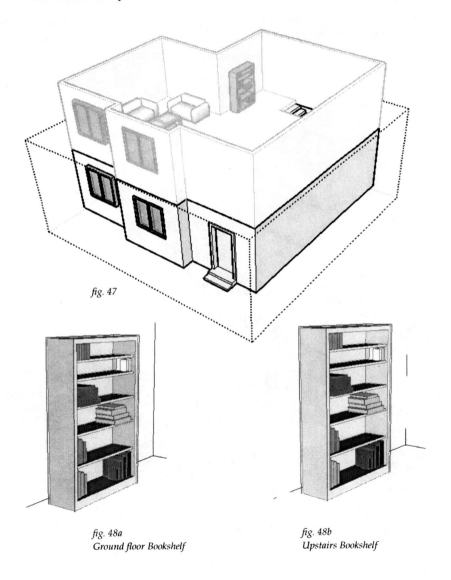

fig. 47

fig. 48a
Ground floor Bookshelf

fig. 48b
Upstairs Bookshelf

Ex. 06 – Layers

1. Open the **Cap04_Ex06.skp** file.

2. Choose **Window/Layers** and create two layers, naming them **Option 1** and **Option 2.**

3. Select the **Table and white chairs** component and place it in layer **Option 1**.

4. Select the **Table and beige chairs** component and place it in layer **Option 2** (*fig. 49*).

5. Make copies of the two components and distribute them throughout the house, as if proposed for the layout of a restaurant (*fig. 50*).

6. Enable and disable the layers to toggle between the proposals (*figs. 51 and 52*).

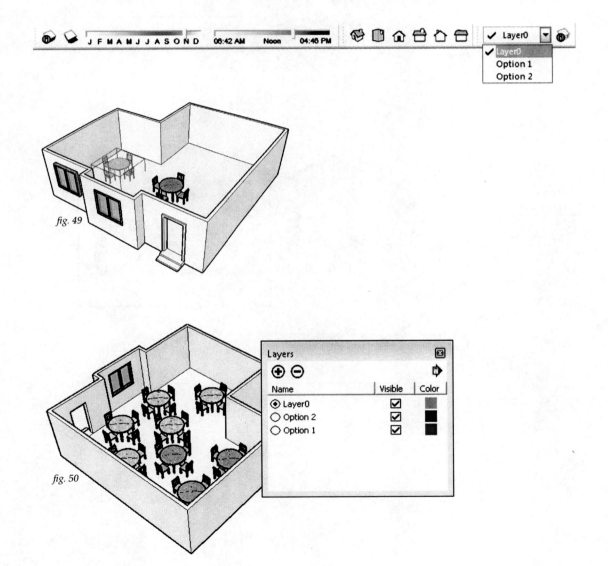

fig. 49

fig. 50

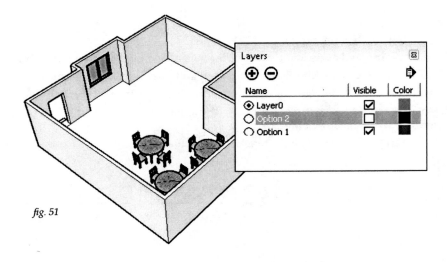

fig. 51

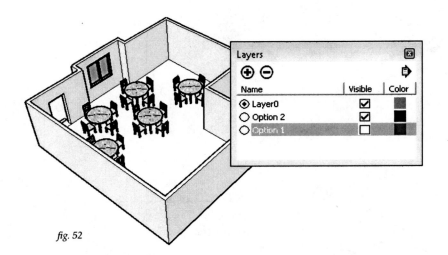

fig. 52

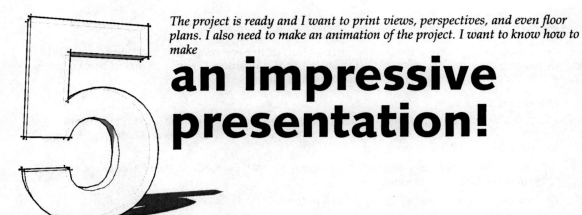

The project is ready and I want to print views, perspectives, and even floor plans. I also need to make an animation of the project. I want to know how to make

an impressive presentation!

SketchUp has a one of a kind graphics style that allows for excellent presentations, in video or on paper. Through the animation resources, it's very easy to make a virtual tour of the project, which can be printed in perspective or also to scale.

What you'll read in this chapter

5.1 Scenes

5.2 How to make an animation

5.3 Printing

5.4 Generating reports

5.1 Scenes

A scene is a SketchUp resource that saves the position of the viewer, texture settings, light and shadows, among others. This information is stored in the **Window/Scenes** menu to be used later, whether it is for printing or for creating an animation clip.

to create a scene

1. Place the viewer in the desired position. Adjust the point of view (with or without a vanishing point), shadows, textures, axes, enable or disable layers, section planes and hidden geometry, to make the view the way you want.

2. Choose **Window/Scenes** and click the + button. SketchUp records all the viewer properties at that moment with a default name.

3. You can change the scene name, typing it in the field.

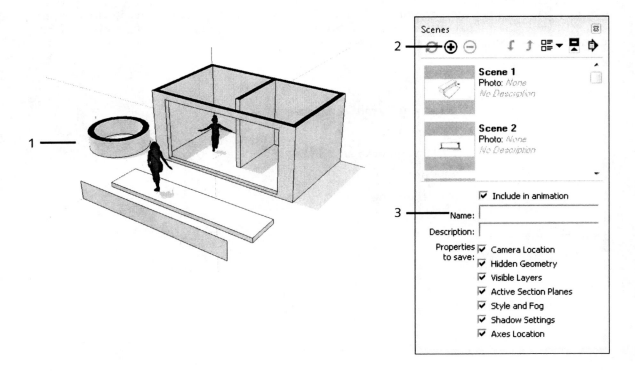

to update a scene

1. Move the viewer position and/or alter the display settings.
2. Choose **Window/Scenes** and select the properties you want to save when updating a scene.

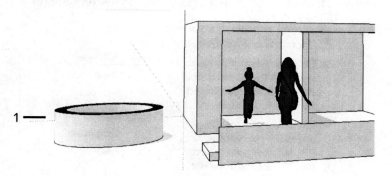

3. Select the scene you want to update (**a**) and click the indicated button (**b**).

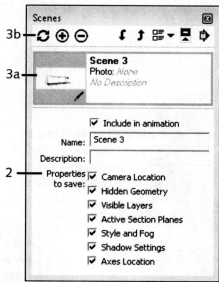

other important options

1. To delete a scene, select it and click on -. Deleting a scene does not delete objects from the drawing.
2. If you want to a particular scene to be part of an animated tour, select it and click on **Include in animation**.

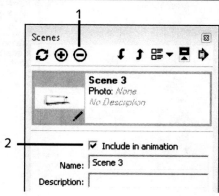

5.2 How to make an animation

SketchUp creates an animation from a sequence of preselected scenes. It's possible to export the animation in video format or as a sequence of numbered images for editing with other software, such as Final Cut and iMovie (Mac), or Adobe Premiere (PC).

choosing scenes of reference

1. Choose **Window/Scenes.**

2. For each scene you want to use in the animation, click on its respective box, **Include in animation.**

3. SketchUp creates the animation according to the order of scenes in the list. Use the buttons with up and down arrows to alter the order.

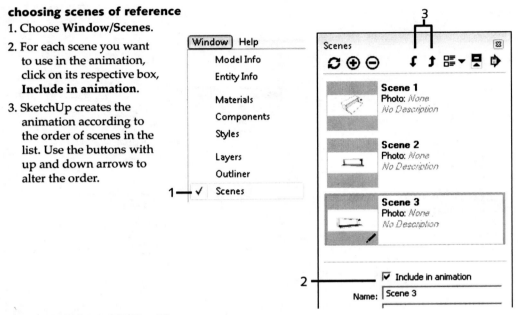

to control the animation times

1. Choose **Window/Model Info/Animation.**

2. Click **Enable scene transitions** checkbox (**a**) to make the animation work. Just below, adjust the duration of the transition between the scenes (**b**).

3. The **Scene Delay** field is used to set the number of seconds SketchUp continues showing a scene without motion.

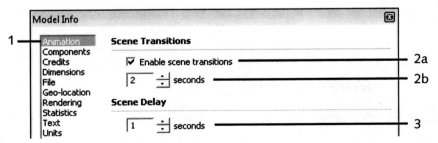

to execute an animation

1. Choose **View/Animation/Play**; after a few seconds, the animation will begin.

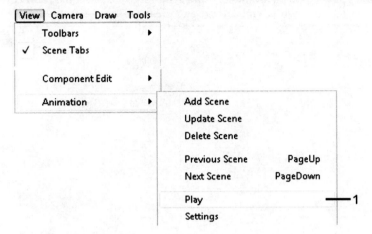

2. To pause or interrupt, click the corresponding buttons, in the **Animation** window that opens after the animation begins.

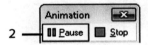

to export an animation as a video

1. To export an animation, it needs to be stopped.

2. Choose **File/Export/Animation/Video....**

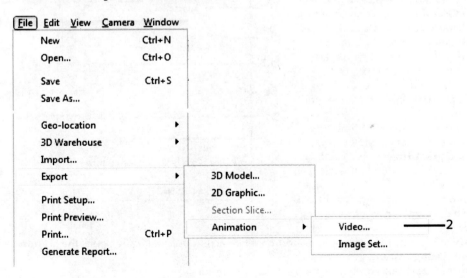

3. Enter a name in the **File name** field.

4. Select the **.avi** format if you want to have an uncompressed video file. Select the **H264 codec/Mp4 file.mp4** format to export a video with a smaller size and great quality.

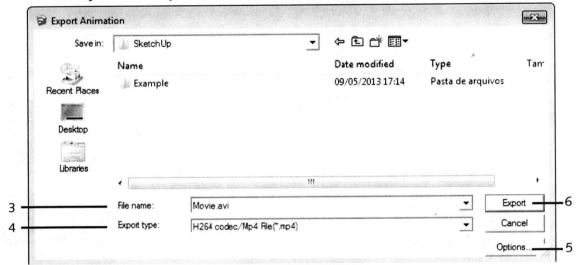

5. Click on **Options...** to configure the details of your animation:

a. **Resolution:** Choose among three resolution sizes or pick **Custom** to use an alternative resolution;

b. **Aspect Ratio:** Choose between **16:9 Wide** or **4:3 Standard** (available when **Resolution** is set to **Custom**);

c. **Frame Size (W x H):** Choose the **Width** and **Height** of the animation window (available when **Aspect Ratio** is set to **Custom**);

d. **Preview Frame Size:** Click to see the actual size of the animation window;

e. **Frame Rate:** Rate of frames per second to be displayed;

f. **Loop to starting scene:** Add a new video sequence, linking the last scene to the first;

g. **Anti-alias rendering:** Enable and adjust the smoothness of rendering objects;

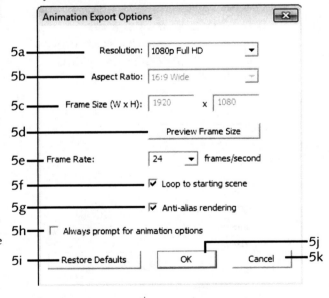

h. **Always prompt for animation options:** When active, automatically opens the **Options** window upon clicking **Export;**

i. **Restore Defaults:** Apply the program default settings;

j. **OK:** Confirm your options;

k. **Cancel:** Cancel your options.

6. To finish, click on **Export.**

5.3 Printing

You can print your project using perspectives or scaled orthogonal projections. The scenes can be used to save a position or viewer settings, facilitating the printing process. In other words, SketchUp prints what is being displayed on the screen at that moment. To print various views in one spread, you need LayOut, a program that is installed with SketchUp Pro. Learn more in **Chapter 7, Build layouts with SketchUp LayOut**, starting on page **178**.

configure the page

1. Choose **File/Print Setup...**.

2. Click on this dropdown list to choose the printer you will be using.

3. In the **Paper** field, choose the paper size used by the printer (A4, Letter...).

4. In the **Orientation** field, select whether the print format will be **Portrait** or **Landscape**.

5. Click on **OK**.

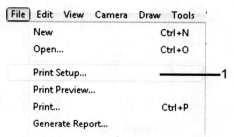

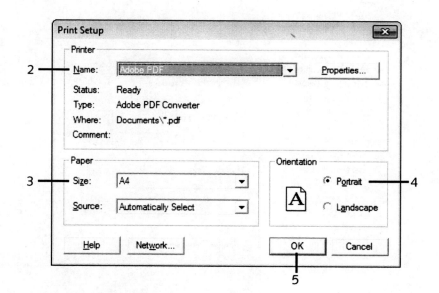

to print an image in perspective, without scaling

1. Choose **File/Print Preview**....

2. If you want an image to occupy the biggest possible size in relation to the printout, click on the **Fit to page** box.

3. To print in another size, uncheck the **Fit to page** box and select the size of the image to be printed, in the **Width** and **Height** fields **(a)**. You may need to use one or more sheets if the size of the spread to be printed is bigger than the size of the sheet. The number of sheets used always appears in the **Tiled Sheet Print Range** field **(b)** and you can even choose which pages created by SketchUp will be actually printed.

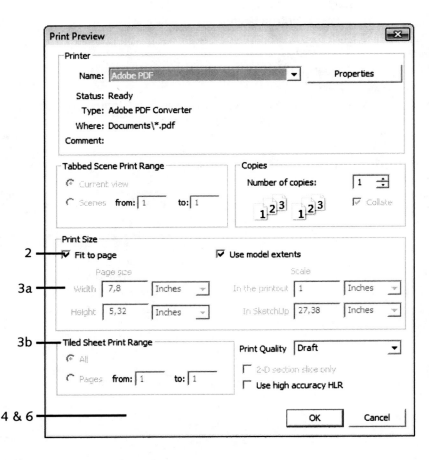

4. Click on **OK** and notice that SketchUp created an image of what will be printed.

5. If you approve it, click on **Print**....

6. SketchUp once again opens the print window for you to alter a detail, if preferred. Click on **OK** to execute printing.

to print a drawing without vanishing points, and set to scale

1. Choose **Camera/Parallel Projection**. Notice that the projection used now is orthogonal.

2. If you want a specific view, use the **Camera/Standard Views** menu; adjust the zoom to fit what you want to print into the window.

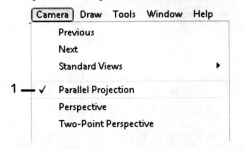

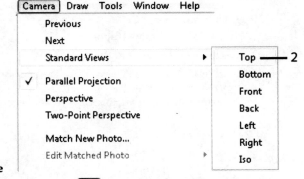

3. Choose **File/Print Preview....**

4. Disable the boxes, **Fit to page (a)** and **Use model extents (b)**.

5. Use the fields, **In the printout** and **In SketchUp** to adjust the scale. In the **In the printout** field, enter a particular size in centimeters (1, for example). In the **In SketchUp** field, enter the equivalent value, to scale (100, for example). In this case, you configured the print to a scale of 1:100.

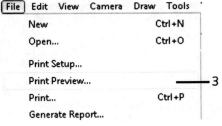

6. Depending on the scaled used, SketchUp may determine that more than one page will be used. You can check this in the field. **Tiled Sheet Print Range.**

7. Click **OK** and notice how SketchUp generated a preview of what will be printed.

8. If you approve it, click on **Print....**

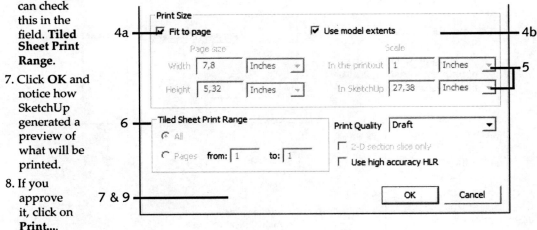

9. SketchUp once again opens a print window for altering details, if preferred. Click on **OK** to finish.

5.4 Generating reports

SketchUp is capable of generating reports with a containing information about components being used in your project. You can choose an HTML report, to view in any browser (Internet Explorer, Firefox, Safari, Chrome, etc.), or create a CSV, to open in programs like Excel.

how to create a report

1. Choose **File/Generate Report....**

2. Select one of the items in the box:

   a. **All model attributes**: If you want a report with all the information from all the objects that are inserted in the model;

   b. **Current selection attributes**: A report is created with all the information on selected objects.

3. Choose an output format for the report:

   a. **Generate HTML file:** To open in any browser (Internet Explorer, Firefox, Safari, etc.);

   b. **Generate CSV file:** To open in spreadsheet editors like Excel and OpenOffice.

4. Next, select the folder (**a**) and enter a name for the file (**b**). Click on **Save** (**c**).

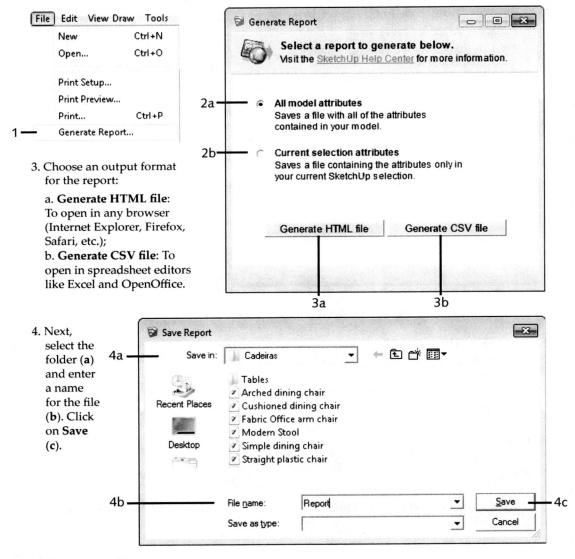

5. A box will appear, asking if you want to open the file you just made. Choose **Yes**.

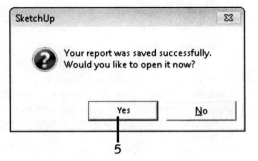

6. SketchUp will open the indicated program through the system to read you file. In the example below, Firefox was opened to read the report created in HTML. Notice how it shows all the information from each component, and also from possible subcomponents.

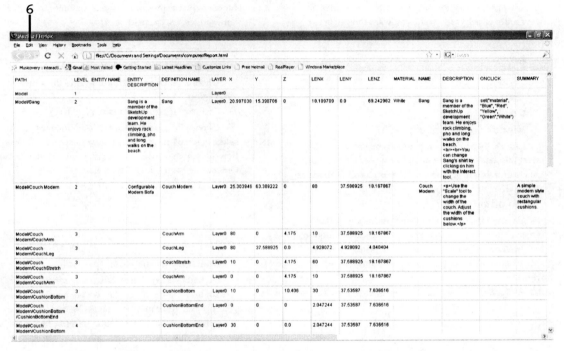

Chapter highlights

Scene

To create a scene (p. 148)

Place the viewer in the desired position, choose **Window/Scenes** menu and click the + button. SketchUp records all the viewer properties in that moment with a default name. You can change the scene name, typing in the **Name** field.

To update a scene (p. 149)

Change the position of the viewer and/or alter the view settings, select the scene you want to update and click on **Update**.

Printing

Configure the page (p. 153)

Choose **File/Print Setup** and in the **Paper** field, select the sheet size that you're using (A4, Letter...); in the **Orientation** field, choose if the print will be made as a **Portrait** or **Landscape**.

To print (p. 154)

Choose **File/Print**; if you want the image in the screen to occupy the biggest size possible in relation to the sheet, click the **Fit to page** box; to print in another size, disable the **Fit to page** box and choose the size in which the image will be printed.

Animation

Choosing scenes of reference (p. 150)

Choose **Window/Scenes** and, for each scene you want to participate in the animation, click on the respective box **Include in animation**.

Control the animation time (p. 150)

Choose **Window/Model Info/Animation** and click on **Enable scene transitions** for the animations to function. Just below, adjust the duration of transition between scenes; the field **Scene Delay** is used for setting the number of seconds SketchUp continues to show a scene without movement.

To execute an animation (p. 151)

Choose **View/Animation/Play** and the animation will begin.

To export an animation (p. 151)

Choose **File/Export/Animation/Video** menu and select the **.mp4** format if you want to open the animation directly in a video player (Windows Media Player, QuickTime Player, RealPlayer, etc.).

Generating reports (p. 156)

SketchUp is capable of generating reports that contain information about the components being used in your project. You can choose an HTML report, to view in any browser (Internet Explorer, Firefox, Safari, etc.), or create a CSV, to open in programs like Excel.

Suggested activities

Ex. 01 – Scenes

1. Open the **Cap05_Ex01.skp** file.

2. Create a scene viewing the house from a front/left view (*fig. 53*).

3. Create another, with parallel projection (**Camera/Parallel Projection** menu) from a frontal view of the house (*fig. 54*).

4. Use the **Camera/Position Camera** menu to position the viewer in front of the house with a height of 49,20" or 1,25m. Create a scene with this point of view (*fig. 55*).

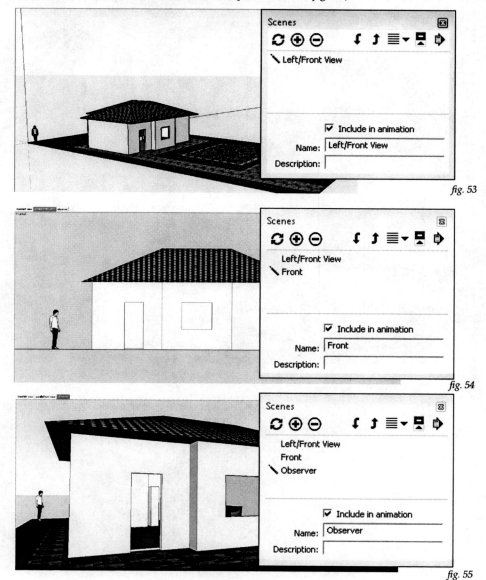

fig. 53

fig. 54

fig. 55

Ex. 02 – Animation

1. Open the **Cap05_Ex02.skp** file.

2. On the **Window/Model Info/Animation** menu, set the transition time to 5 seconds, with 0 seconds delay between the scenes (*fig. 56*).

3. Choose **View/Animation/Play** to see a preview of your animation (*fig. 57*).

4. Click the **Stop** button to stop the preview (*fig. 58*).

5. Choose **File/Export/Animation/Video...** and create an animation in **.mp4** format with 720p HD Resolution, and 10 frames per second (*fig. 59*).

6. Watch your animation in Windows Media Player or Quicktime Player (*fig. 60*).

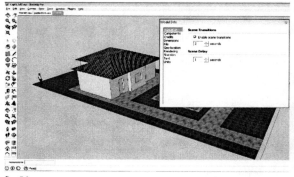

fig. 56

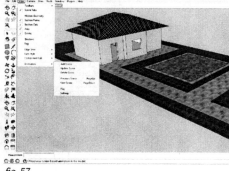

fig. 57

fig. 58

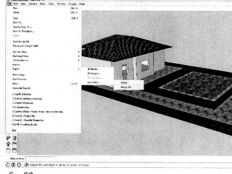

fig. 59

fig. 60

Ex. 03 – Print to scale

1. Open the **Cap05_Ex03.skp** file.

2. Place the viewer in top view and change the projection to parallel (**Camera/Parallel Projection** menu).

3. Choose **File/Print Setup...** and configure the page for A4 format, with Portrait orientation (*fig. 61*).

4. On the **File/Print** menu, print in to a scale of 1:125, with **High Definition** print quality (*fig. 62*).

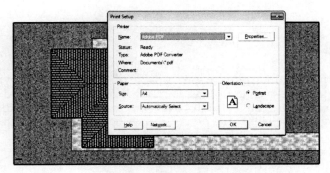

fig. 61

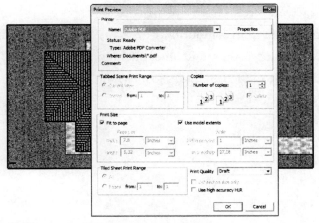

fig. 62

Ex. 04 – Generating reports

1. Open the **Cap05_Ex04.skp** file.

2. Create a report using the **File/Generate Report...** menu.

3. Open the file in a program, such as Internet Explorer or Firefox, and see the result.

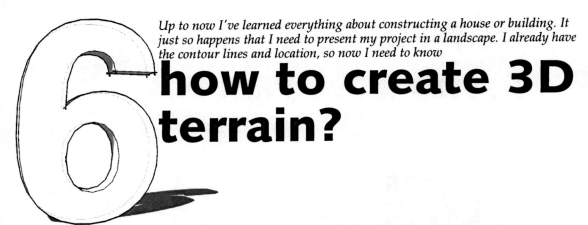

Up to now I've learned everything about constructing a house or building. It just so happens that I need to present my project in a landscape. I already have the contour lines and location, so now I need to know

how to create 3D terrain?

In this chapter you will learn everything SketchUp is capable of in terms of terrain modeling. You can start a terrain from scratch, or use contour lines to create it. You'll learn to modify and create plateaus, ramps, and other elements. You'll also discover how to apply an image directly to the terrain, to see how the topography changes the perception we have in an urban site, for example.

What you'll read in this chapter

6.1 How to activate terrain tools

6.2 Create terrain from a plane

6.3 Terrain from contour lines

6.4 Plateaus, ramps, and other alterations

6.5 How to attach an image to a terrain

6.1 How to activate terrain tools

how to activate terrain tools for creating a terrain

1. Choose **Window/Preferences**.

2. Click on **Extensions**.

3. Enable the box for **Sandbox Tools**.

4. Click on **OK**.

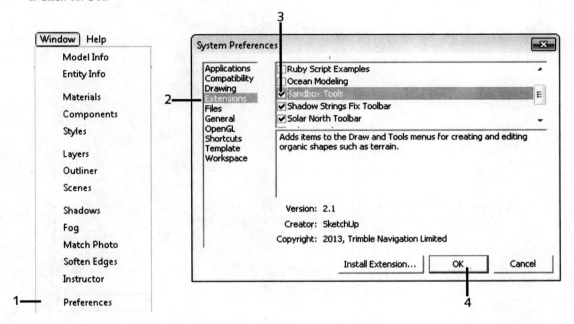

6.2 Create terrain from a plane

SketchUp has a tool called **From Scratch** that serves to create a flat rectangular grid. You can modify the height of the vertices of this mesh, creating elevations and depressions in the terrain.

how to create the terrain base

1. Choose **Draw/Sandbox/From Scratch**.

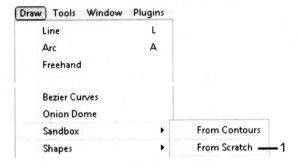

2. In the **Measurements** toolbar, type the specific amount for spacing between the rectangles in the mesh and press **Enter**.

3. Click on the point where you want to start the base of the terrain.

4. Move the cursor to indicate the lateral size of the terrain and click to confirm.

5. Move the cursor in the other direction and click again to finish the base.

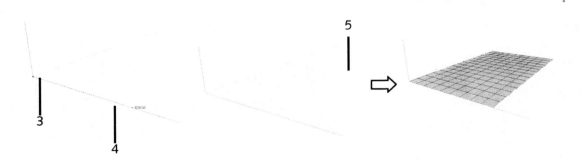

how to create hills and valleys in your terrain

1. Select the terrain to be worked.
2. Right-click over it and then click **Explode**. You can also choose **Edit Group**, if you don't want to ungroup the terrain.

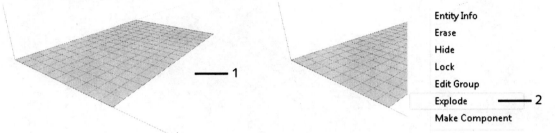

3. Choose **Tools/Sandbox/Smoove**.
4. In the **Measurements** toolbar, enter the sculpting radius for the tool.
5. Click on the point of the terrain you want to sculpt and drag the cursor up and down until you get the result you wanted.
6. Click to confirm the ground sculpting.

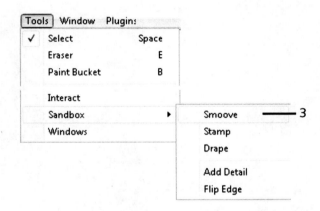

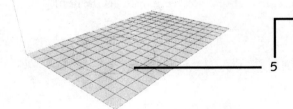

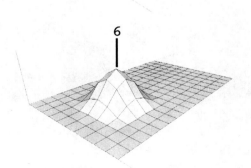

how to modify the height of selected vertices

1. Select the terrain vertices that will have their height modified (to select vertices in different parts of the terrain press the **shift** key).

2. Choose **Tools/Sandbox/Smoove**.

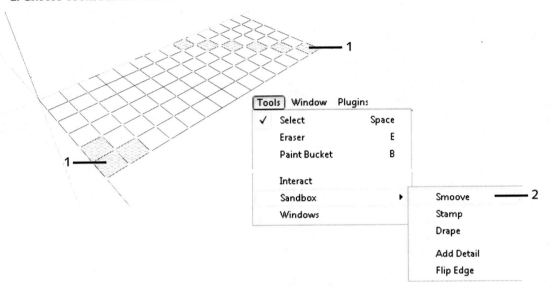

3. In the **Measurements** toolbar, enter the sculpting radius for the tool.

4. Click on a point of the terrain and drag the cursor up and down until you get the result you wanted.

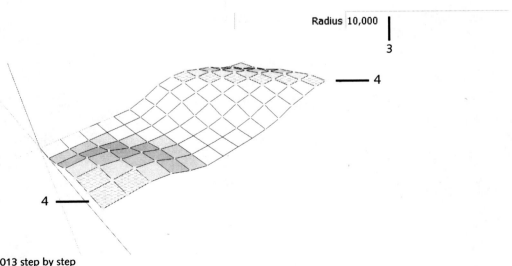

other interesting options

1. To create a vertex in any space between vertices on the terrain, choose **Tools/ Sandbox/Add Detail** and then click on a point on the terrain.

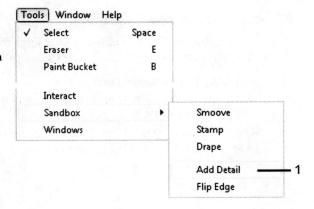

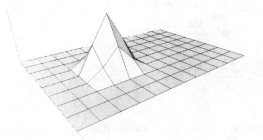

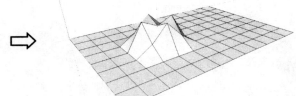

2. To invert the direction of a vertex on the terrain, choose **Tools/Sandbox/Flip Edge**, then click on the vertex that you want to alter.

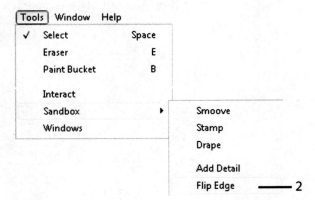

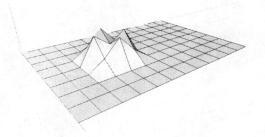

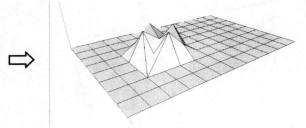

6.3 Terrain from contour lines

You can draw or import ready-made contour lines from another drawing program. SketchUp is able to transform these curves into 3D terrain that can be modified later.

preparing the contour lines

To begin making terrain from curves, you need to place each curve at its respective height. To make this happen, do the following:

1. Select an entire contour line. To save time, you can triple-click on any point of the contour line.

2. On the **Edit toolbar**, choose the **Move** tool.

3. Click on the contour line and drag it until it reaches the desired height.

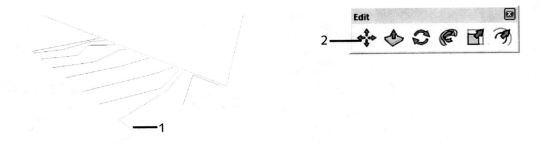

4. If preferred, enter a value in the **Measurements** toolbar after clicking to make the contour line rise or descend with an exact dimension.

5. Repeat this procedure until all the contour lines are adjusted.

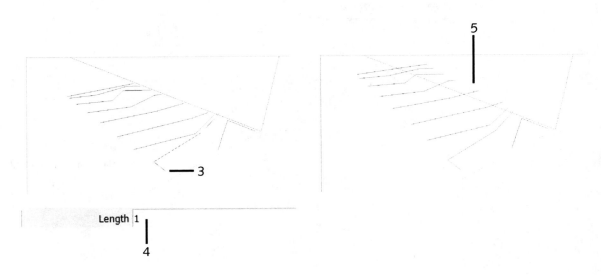

how to create a terrain from curves

1. Select all the contour lines that will make up the terrain.

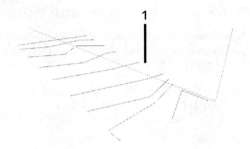

2. Choose **Draw/Sandbox/From Contours** and the terrain will be created automatically.

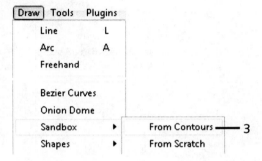

3. You can move the terrain or create a layer for it, for the purpose of altering it without disturbing the original contour lines.

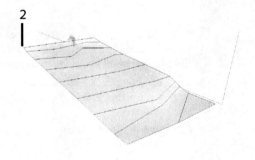

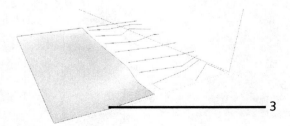

6.4 Plateaus, ramps, and other alterations

After the terrain is ready, you can modify it with some interesting tools. It's possible to create plateaus and ramps for accommodating buildings, representing roads, and other changes in the topography. There is also a tool for modifying the texture applied to a part of the terrain.

how to create a plateau

1. Draw a polygon that has the format of a plateau and place it below, or above the terrain.
2. Select the face of the polygon that will serve as a reference for the plateau.

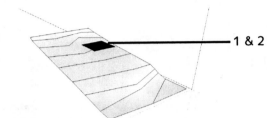

3. Choose **Tools/Sandbox/Stamp**.

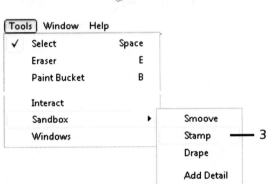

4. In the **Measurements** toolbar, enter the reference amount so SketchUp can adjust the plateau on the terrain, then press **Enter**.
5. Click on the terrain and drag the cursor up or down until you find the ideal position for your plateau.
6. Click once again to finish.

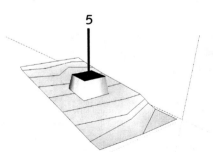

NOTE There is no way to enter a precise height value as you create a plateau.

how to create a ramp

1. Draw a polygon with the format of a ramp and position it below or above the terrain.

2. With the **Move** tool, move one of the edges of the polygon in a vertical direction, up or down, indicating the incline of the ramp. If you prefer, you can enter a value in the **Measurements** toolbar to change the height of the polygon vertex.

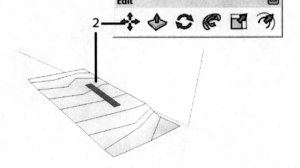

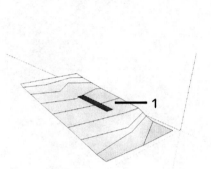

3. Select the face of the polygon to serve as a reference for the ramp.

4. Choose **Tools/Sandbox/Stamp**.

5. In the **Measurements** toolbar, enter the reference value for SketchUp to adjust the ramp on the terrain. Next, press **Enter**.

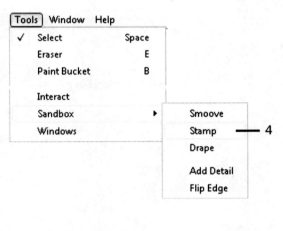

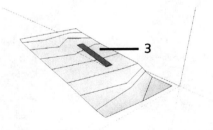

6. Click on the terrain and drag the cursor up or down until you reach the ideal position for your ramp.

7. Click once again to finish.

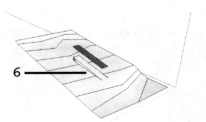

NOTE It's not possible to enter precise height for creating the plateau.

how to drape a polygon and/or lines on terrain

1. Draw a polygon and/or reference lines and position them below or above the terrain.

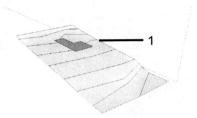

2. Select the elements that will serve as a reference for the drawing.

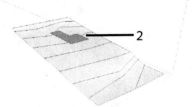

3. Choose **Tools/Sandbox/Drape**.

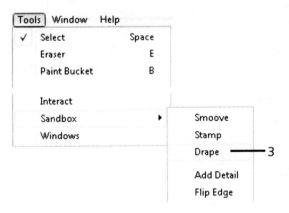

4. Click on the terrain to confirm. Notice that your terrain was marked starting from the polygon projection.

6.5 How to attach an image to a terrain

After creating a terrain, we often want to project an image onto it, possibly an aerial photo, a satellite image or even a hand sketched drawing. Next, you'll learn how to do this.

preparing objects to be attached to an image

To stamp an image on a terrain, you'll need:

1. A ready terrain, modified or not. This terrain should be in a different position than the contour lines that serve as a reference for your creation.

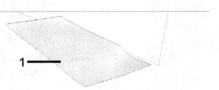

2. An image to be attached, should be imported using the **Import** option.

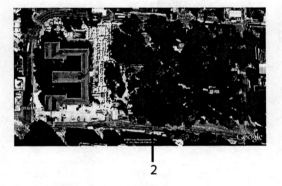

3. The image should be above or below the terrain. Both the image and the terrain should be adjusted into position and size in a way that ensures the application will be perfect.

how to apply an image

1. Right-click on the terrain and choose **Explode**.
2. Right-click on the image and choose **Explode**.

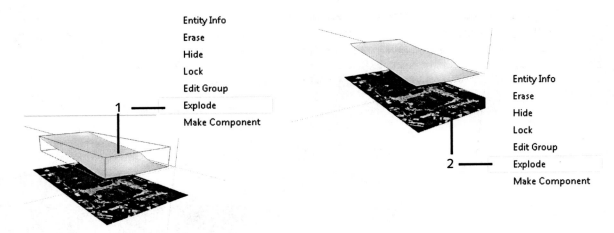

3. Choose **Window/Material** and click on the **Sample Paint**.
4. Click on any point of the image.
5. Click on any point of the terrain. Notice how the image is applied.

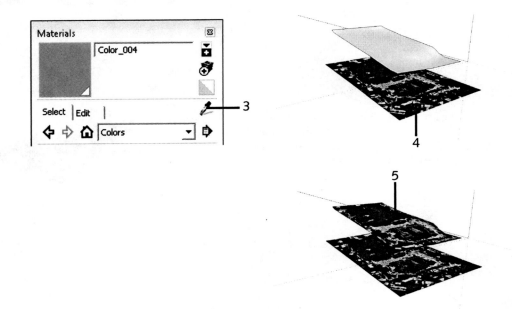

Chapter highlights

Activate terrain tools (p. 163)

Choose **Window/Preferences**, click on **Extensions** and activate the **Sandbox** tools.

Terrain from contour lines (p. 168)

Select all the contour lines that will make up the terrain; choose **From Contours** and the terrain will be automatically created.

Create terrain from a plane

How to create a terrain base (p. 164)

Choose **Tool/Sandbox/From Scratch**; in the **Measurements** toolbar, enter the amount of spacing to place between the mesh rectangles and press **Enter**. Click on the point where you want to start the base of the terrain; drag the cursor to indicate the lateral size of the terrain and click to confirm; drag the cursor in the other direction and click once more to finish the base.

Create hills and valleys in your terrain (p. 165)

Select the terrain to be sculpted, right-click with the cursor over the terrain and choose **Explode**; choose **Tools/Sandbox/Smoove** tool; enter the radius sculpting for the movement of the ground you'll make next. Click on the point of the terrain that you want to move and drag the cursor up and down until you reach the result you wanted. Click to confirm.

Plateaus, ramps, and other alterations

How to create a plateau (p. 170)

Draw a polygon in the format of a plateau and position it below, or above the terrain; select the face of the polygon that will serve as a reference for the plateau and choose the **Stamp** tool. In the **Measurements** toolbar, enter a reference amount for SketchUp to adjust the plateau on the terrain; next, press **Enter**; click on the terrain and drag the cursor up or down until you find the ideal position for your plateau; click once more to finish.

How to create a ramp (p. 171)

Draw a polygon with the format of a ramp; move one of the edges of the polygon in a vertical direction, up or down, indicating the incline of the ramp. Select the face of the polygon that will serve as a reference for the ramp and then choose the **Stamp** tool. In the **Measurements** toolbar, enter the reference amount for SketchUp to adjust the ramp on the terrain, then press **Enter**; click on the terrain and drag the cursor up or down until you find the ideal position for your ramp; click once more to finish.

Drape a polygon and/or lines on a terrain (p. 172)

Draw a polygon and/or reference lines and select them; choose the **Drape** tool and then click on the terrain to confirm.

How to attach an image to terrain

How to attach an image (p. 173)

Right-click on the terrain and choose the **Explode** option; right-click on the image and choose the **Explode** option; on the **Window/Materials** menu, choose the **Sample Paint** tool. Click on any point of the image and then click on any point of the terrain.

Suggested activities

Ex. 01 – Create terrain

1. Open the **Cap06_Ex01.skp** file (*fig. 63*).

2. Select each contour line and use the **Move** tool to move them to the desired height.

3. In our example, the first curve was raised 8m or 315", the next 7m or 275", and the rest in the same way (*fig. 64*).

4. Select all the contour lines and use the **From Contours** tool to create a terrain (*fig. 65*).

5. Use the **Move** tool to move the terrain you created. Notice that the original curves remain in the drawing (*fig. 66*).

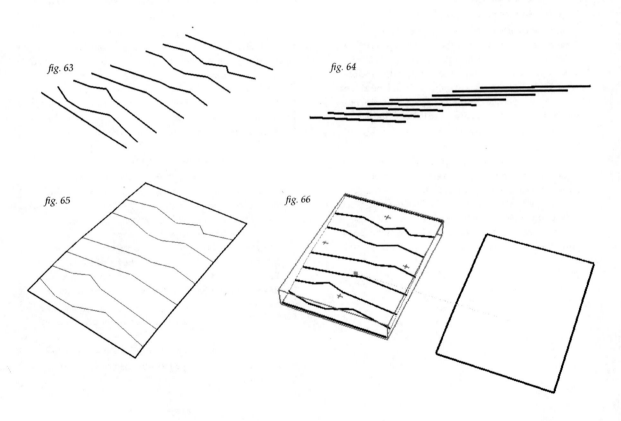

fig. 63

fig. 64

fig. 65

fig. 66

Ex. 02 – Editing terrain

1. Open the **Cap06_Ex02.skp** file.

2. Select the face of the circle and use the **Drape** tool. Click on the terrain and observe the result (*fig. 67*).

3. Select the face of the rectangle, which will serve a reference for the plateau; choose the **Stamp** tool to adjust the measurement to 39" or 1m. Click on the terrain and move the cursor to set to the desired height (*figs. 68* and *69*).

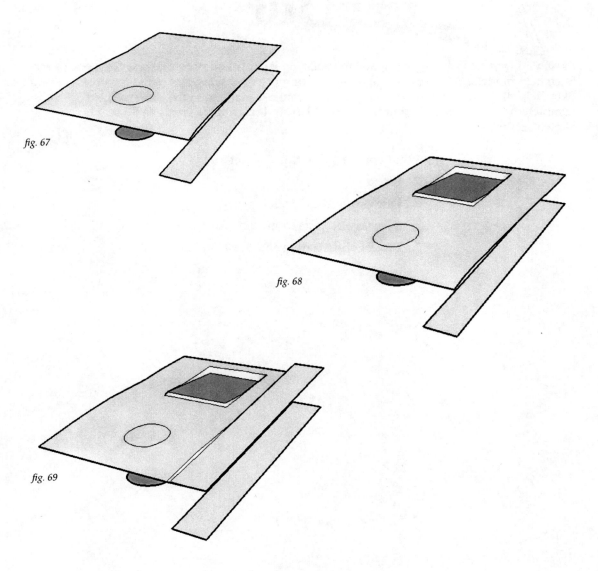

fig. 67

fig. 68

fig. 69

I have many projects and would like to create layouts with some of them. Sometimes I need a lot of layouts with several views of the same project. I don't want to use other programs, mostly because they tell me I can

build layouts with SketchUp LayOut

SketchUp LayOut is a program made for building layouts and presentations from one or more SketchUp models. You can have, in a file, one or more design layouts with viewports coming from SketchUp files that are updated every time a change is made to to the original file. LayOut is a complete program, independent from SketchUp, and distributed freely to those who buy SketchUp Pro.

What you'll read in this chapter

7.1 Setup

7.2 Drawing and edit tools

7.3 Inserting projects from SketchUp

7.4 Project organization and presentation

7.1 Setup

LayOut, as mentioned before, is completely independent from SketchUp and for this reason it has its own configurations for page size, units, and templates. The following is a list of the main setup adjustments for the program.

to configure the page and the margins

1. Choose **File/Document Setup....**
2. In the window that opens, click on **Paper.**
3. In the indicated field, choose from among the default paper sizes.
4. Select the orientation of the paper, **Landscape** or **Portrait.**

5. If you want a different paper size from the ones indicated in **3**, enter the desired **Width** and **Height.**
6. Choose a color for the paper, by clicking and dragging the color from the **Color** window.
7. Click the **Print Paper Color** box if you want to print the color of paper chosen in **6**.
8. Click this button to activate and deactivate the page margins.
9. In these fields, set the margin sizes for each side of the pages.
10. Choose a color for the margin, by clicking and dragging from the **Color** window.
11. Click on the **Print Margin Lines** box if you want to print the color of the margin selected in **10**.
12. In **Edit Quality** choose the display quality of the viewports on the screen.
13. In **Output Quality** choose the display quality of the viewports for printing.
14. Click on **Close** to save and close the changes.

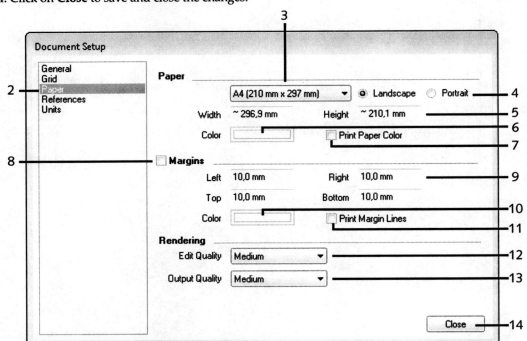

how to adjust units

1. Choose **File/Document Setup….**

2. In the window that opens, click on **Units**.

3. In the **Format** field, choose from among the **Decimal** format (divides units in decimals) and **Fractional** format (divides units in fractions).

4. In this field, choose the units used as a reference on the page.

5. In the **Precision** field, set the number of decimal places to be used.

6. Click on **Close** to close and save the changes.

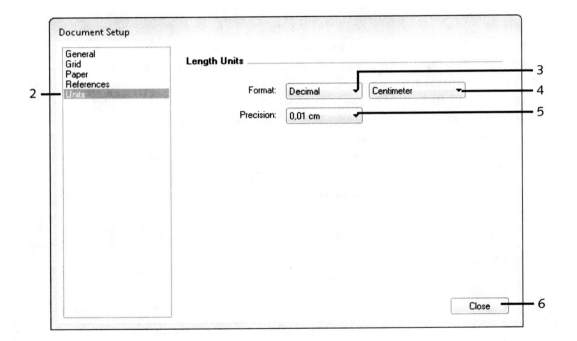

to save a document as a template

1. Choose **File/Save As Template....**

2. In the window that opens, enter a name for the template to be created.

3. Choose a folder in which to save the template: **My Templates** or **Default Templates**.

4. Click on **OK**.

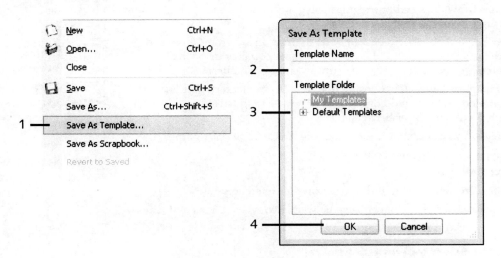

7.2 Drawing and edit tools

LayOut drawing tools are very simple. It's possible to draw using measurements, but keep in mind these tools should be used to create margins, indicator stamps, and not for project drawings.

drawing tools

1. **Lines:** Draw lines and/or irregular polygons. Click for each polygon vertex desired. Press the **ESC** key to finish.

2. **Arc:** You'll choose between four ways to draw an arc: from center and radius, from two ends and center, from three points or using the Pie method (center and radius with surrounded by contour lines).

3. **Rectangles:** Allows for choosing from four types: the rectangle itself, and **Rounded, Bulged,** and **Lozenge,** which create rounded sides or vertices with small differences between them.

4. **Circles:** You can use these tools to create circles or ovals.

5. **Polygon:** Draw regular polygons.

6. **Text:** Create texts.

7. **Label:** Create texts with indicator arrows for reference.

8. **Dimensions:** Allows for choosing between two types: **Linear** and **Angular.**

	Join	
1	Lines	▸
2	Arcs	▸
3	Rectangles	▸
4	Circles	▸
5	Polygon	
6	Text	
7	Label	
8	Dimensions	▸

using the Select tool for editing

1. **Stretch** or **Shrink:** Choose the object that you want to reshape and place the cursor near the point to be altered. When the cursor becomes a reshape arrow, click and drag to change the size of the object.

2. **Move:** Choose the object that you want to move. When the cursor takes the shape of a cross, click and drag to move it.

3. **Rotate:** Click on the object you intend to rotate and position the cursor over the central red circle; when the cursor takes the shape of circular arrows, click and drag to indicate the rotation that you want.

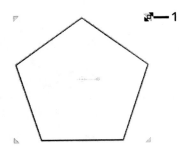
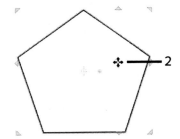
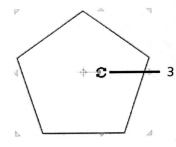

other object editing tools

1. On the **Tools** menu:

   a. **Erase**: To delete lines and faces;

   b. **Style**: Allows for selecting the color of one object and using it for another;

   c. **Split**: Allows for splitting an object by clicking anywhere on its edge;

   d. **Join**: Allows for joining objects.

Tools

1a — Erase

1b — Style

1c — Split

1d — Join

2. On the **Arrange** menu:

   a. **Bring to Front**: Place the object above all the others;

   b. **Bring Forward**: Place the object one level above;

   c. **Send Backward**: Place the object one level below;

   d. **Send to Back**: Place the object below all the others;

   e. **Align**: Control the alignment options of the objects;

   f. **Space**: Control the spacing between the objects;

   g. **Center**: Control the position of objects in relation to the page;

   h. **Flip**: Invert the object (horizontally or vertically).

Arrange

2a — Bring to Front

2b — Bring Forward

2c — Send Backward

2d — Send to Back

2e — Align ▶

2f — Space ▶

2g — Center ▶

2h — Flip ▶

7.3 Inserting projects from SketchUp

This is the most important part of working with LayOut. You'll insert one or more views from your project using a feature called viewport. It's possible to create viewports from any SketchUp file; each one of them has its own display and presentation settings, as you'll see ahead.

how to insert a SketchUp project in a new LayOut file

1. Into the SketchUp file choose **File/Send to LayOut**.

2. LayOut will open a new window. Choose the file: this can be a template (**a**) or an existing LayOut file (**b**).

3. Click on **Open**.

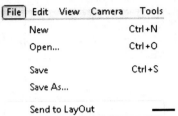

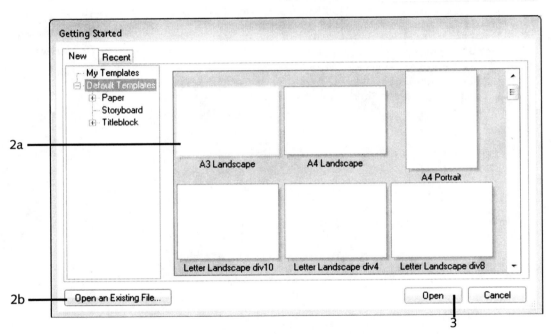

another way to insert a SketchUp project into an existing LayOut file

1. Open the LayOut file that will receive the project from SketchUp.

2. Choose **File/Insert....**

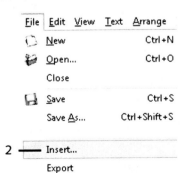

3. In the dialog box, select the SketchUp file to be inserted (**a**), then click on **Open** (**b**).

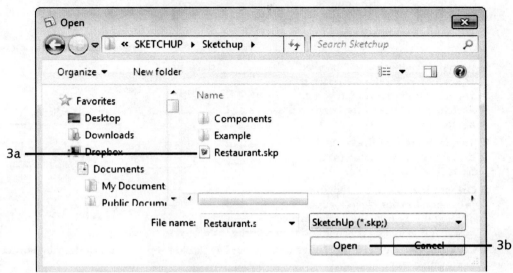

how to change the shape of the viewport
1. Draw a object to serve as a reference clip of the viewport.
2. Pressing the **Shift** key, select the two objects (viewport and object).
3. Choose **Edit/Create Clipping Mask**. Notice how the viewport was clipped.

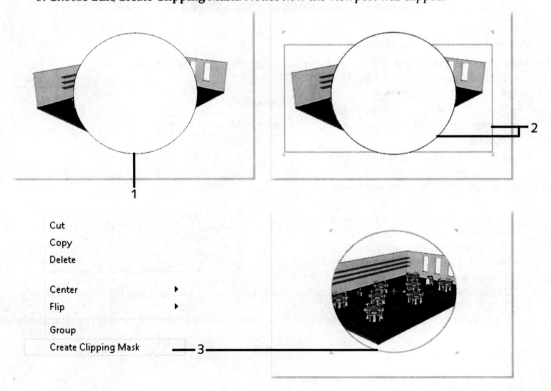

how to edit the view of a viewport

The commands for editing the view of a viewport are in the **SketchUp Model** window, on the **View** tab:

1. **Scenes:** Click to choose which scene from the original file will be used as a reference for the viewport. If you don't have a recorded scene, SketchUp will use the last one used as a reference.

2. **Standard Views:** Click on the dropdown list to choose from SketchUp default views.

3. **Ortho:** Click to add a orthogonal projection to your view (**a**); upon clicking this button, the dropdown list beside it is activated (**b**) so you can choose the scale used in the viewport.

4. Click on **Preserve Scale on Resize** if you want LayOut to keep the scale of the viewport the same when you change its size.

5. **Shadows:** Click this button to enable shadows projections in the viewport (**a**). When activated, this button enables settings for hour (**b**) and date (**c**) of shadow projections.

6. **Fog:** Click this button to activate the use of fog in this viewport (**a**). To function correctly, the fog should be enabled in the original file. When active, you can choose between setting a specific color for the fog (**b**), or use the background color of the document (**c**).

to edit the style of a viewport

The view edit commands for a viewport are in the SketchUp Model window, on the **Styles** tab:

1. Click this button to choose between the styles in your file or those from the program library.

2. In this area, you'll click to open folders containing styles, just like activating the style you want to apply.

3. Click on these buttons to change the view of the window indicated in **2**. The first button (**a**) organizes the window as a list and the second (**b**), in large icons.

4. **Background:** Click to enable and disable the background of your project. It's more effective in **Vector** style displays.

5. **Line Weight:** Type an amount in this box to determine the thickness of the lines of your viewport.

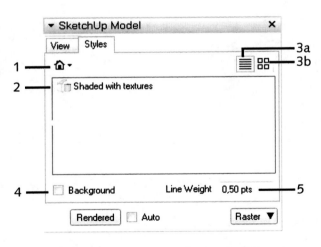

render settings of a viewport

The render settings of a viewport are found in the lower portion of the SketchUp Model window:

1. Click on **Auto** to enable or disable the automatic rendering of the viewport.

2. Click on **Render** to produce the viewport. This button is only active when the **Auto** box is disabled.

3. This symbol indicates that the viewport has been updated and should be rendered once again.

4. Click this button to choose between the viewport render options: **Vector (a)**, recommended for viewports without styles applied; **Raster (b)**, for viewports with styles and **Hybrid (c)**, which mixes the options of the other two.

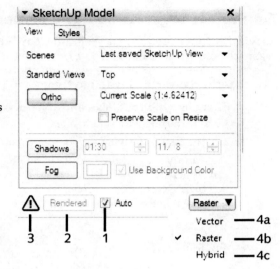

7.4 Project organization and presentation

As with various other design programs, LayOut has ways of making it easier to produce and organize your presentations. You can create each layout in a page and organize the drawing objects in layers to improve the visibility control. Just remember that these resources (pages and layers) aren't coordinated with the scenes and layers from SketchUp.

to change the font, size and style of a text

1. Select the text you want to alter.

2. In the **Text Style** window, you can choose the preferred changes:

    a. **Family:** Choose the font of the selected text;
    b. **Typeface:** Allows you to change the type of the text (normal, bold, italic);
    c. **Size:** Determine the size of the text body.

3. Notice that the text was modified.

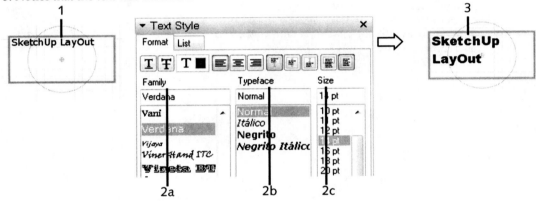

text alignment options

1. Select the text you want to alter.

2. In the **Text Style** window, you can choose your
    preferred alignment:

    a. **Align Left:** Align the selected text to the left;
    b. **Center:** Position the text in the center of the box;
    c. **Align Right:** Align the selected text to the right.

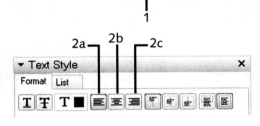

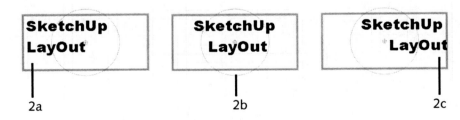

how to change the text color

1. Select the text you want to alter.

2. In the **Text Style** window, click on the indicated button.

3. In the **Colors** window, choose the desired color. Notice how the text was changed to the selected color.

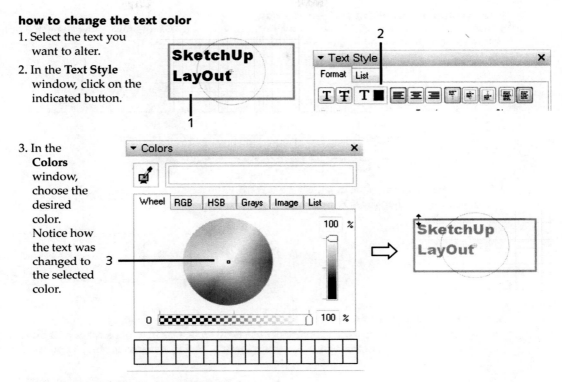

to make a dimension in a viewport

1. Confirm that the viewport is set to a standard view and parallel projection is turned on.

2. Choose the **Dimension** tool.

3. Click on the starting point of the measurement (**a**), move the mouse and click on the endpoint to be measured (**b**); move the mouse to establish the dimension placement and click to finish (**c**).

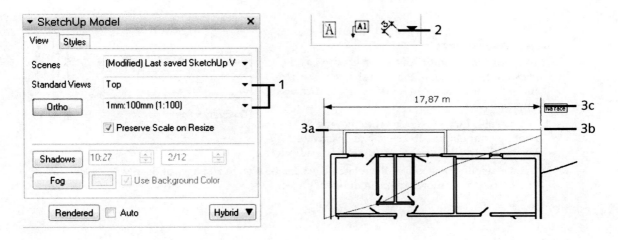

how to alter a dimension text – and undo

1. To force the alteration of a dimension value, double-click over it (**a**); next, enter the value or text you want in place of the original value (**b**). To confirm, press **Enter**.

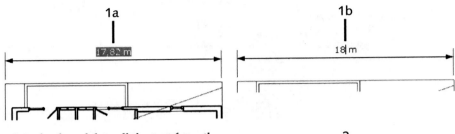

2. To show the original value, delete all the text from the **Dimension** and then press **Enter**.

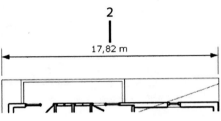

how to use the layers in LayOut

You can use layers to control the visibility of objects on a page, as in various other programs. You can also share a layer. In this way, everything that's placed in a shared layer can appear in all the pages of the file.

to create and rename a layer

1. In the **Layers** window, click the indicated button. A new layer is created.

2. To rename it, double-click over the name. Enter the new name of the layer.

other layer settings

1. To change the visibility of a layer, choose **Layers**, click on the eye icon of the layer that you want to make invisible. To make it visible again, click on the same icon.

2. You can also lock a layer, to avoid moving or altering your objects. To activate of deactivate layer locking, click on the corresponding padlock icon.

3. Upon activating this option, the related layer can be seen in all pages of the file, in order to allow you to use one or more objects in different pages.

how to use pages and the presentation

You can use the pages as printouts of your project, or also as a full screen presentation. Each page can show or not show objects placed in shared layers.

to create, rename and control the visibility of a page

1. To create a new page, Choose **Pages** window and click on the indicated icon. Notice how a new page has been created.

2. To rename a page, double-click on its name and enter a new one.

3. Click the indicated button to allow the indicated page to be a part of the presentation.

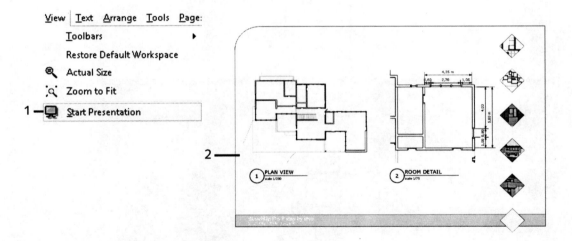

how to execute a presentation

1. Choose **View/Start Presentation**.

2. Your LayOut pages will appear, occupying the full screen. To switch between pages, use the arrow keys.

3. To exit full screen, press **ESC**.

how to use and record notes made during a presentation

1. When in presentation mode, you can use the cursor to make notations on the page. When you click and drag, it's as if you were using a pen.

2. When you return to the normal screen mode (pressing **ESC**), LayOut will ask if you want to save the notes you made; choose **Yes**, if you want to keep the notes on the drawing.

3. Notice that the notes are saved in a new layer, named with the date of notation.

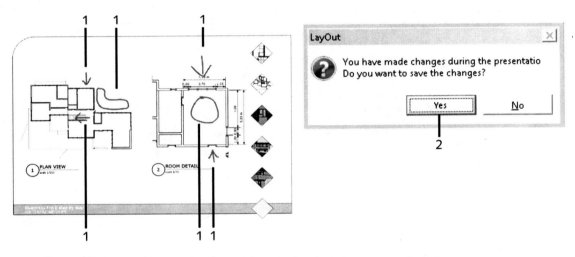

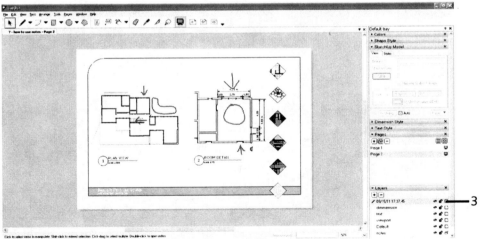

Chapter highlights

Setup

Page and margins (p. 179)

Choose **File/Document Setup...** . Next, click on **Paper**; configure the size and orientation of the paper, the color of the paper and the margins and the resolution of images in printing.

How to adjust units (p. 180)

Choose **File/Document Setup...** and click on **Units**; choose which unit will be used and define its format; in the **Precision** field, establish how many decimal places will be used.

Save a document as a template (p. 181)

Choose **File/Save as Template**; enter the name of the template to be created; choose in which folder to save the model: **My Templates** or **Default Templates** and click **OK.**

Drawing and edit tools

drawing tools (p. 182)

Use the **Line, Arc, Rectangle, Circles**, and **Polygon** tools. You can use the **Text** and **Label** tools to write.

object editing tools (p. 183)

To edit objects, use the **Select** tool to move, rotate, stretch or shrink any object. The commands, **Bring to Front, Bring Forward, Send Backward**, and **Send to Back**, change the position of an object in relation to the others.

You can arrange the various objects with the **Align, Space**, and **Center** commands; use **Flip** to invert the object.

Inserting projects from SketchUp

Insert SketchUp project into a new file in LayOut (p. 184)

Choose **File/Send to LayOut**; in LayOut, choose the file (this can be a template) where the viewport will be inserted and click on **Open**.

How to change the shape of the viewport (p. 185)

Draw a polygon to serve as a clipping reference for the viewport, and pressing the **Shift** key, select the two objects (viewport and polygon); choose **Edit/Make Clipping Mask**.

How to edit the view of a viewport (p. 186)

You can edit the view of a viewport from the **View** tab; the presentation styles, from the **Styles** tab; shadows and fog effect in the **Shadow** and **Fog** tabs.

Organization and presentation

Use layers in LayOut (p. 190)

You can use the layers to control the visibility of objects on a page, as in other programs. You can share one or more layers. Everything that is placed in a shared layer can appear on all the pages of a file.

How to use pages and presentation (p. 192)

You can use the pages as printouts of your project, or also as a full screen presentation. Each page can show/hide objects placed in shared layers.

Suggested activities

Ex. 01 – Template configurations

1. Open the **Cap07_Ex01.layout** file.

2. Configure the units of the document, using the **File/Document Setup...** menu (*fig. 70*).

3. Save the file as a template.

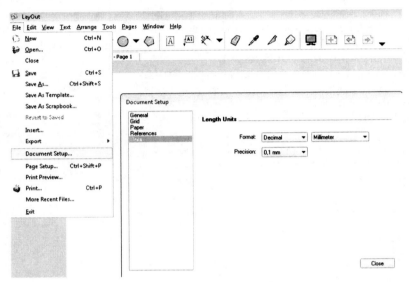

fig. 70

Ex. 02 – Stamp

1. Open the **Cap07_Ex02.layout** file.

2. Open the file, **Cap07_Ex02.pdf**, which contains the reference drawing.

3. Use the LayOut drawing tools to create a stamp like the one in the reference file (*fig. 71*).

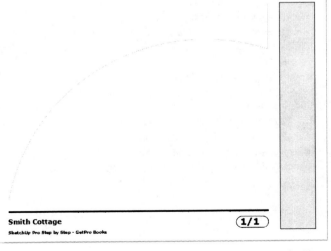

fig. 71

Ex. 03 – Insert file from SketchUp

1. Open the file, **Cap07_Ex03.layout**.

2. Insert three viewports from the file, **Cap07_Ex03.skp**, as shown in *fig. 72*:

   a. Make an external viewport, in **perspective**;
   b. Make a viewport in **front view**, non perspective, to scale 1:250;
   c. Make a viewport in **top view**, also non perspective and to scale, 1:250.

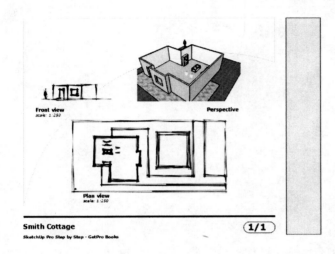

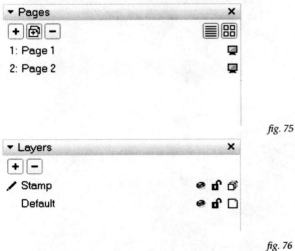

fig. 72

Ex. 04 – Pages and layers

1. Open the file, **Cap07_Ex04.layout**.

2. Create a new page and name it **Page 2** (*fig. 75*).

3. Create a new layer and name it **Stamp** (*fig. 76*).

fig. 75

fig. 76

4. Place the objects (lines, rectangles, etc.) that make up the stamp in the **Stamp** layer.

5. Share the **Stamp** layer (*fig. 77*) and observe how the elements of the stamp appear on the other page (*fig. 78*).

6. On **Page 2**, insert new viewports from the file, **Cap07_Ex03.skp**, to complete the presentation of your project (*fig. 79*).

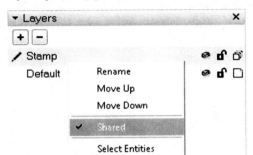

fig. 77

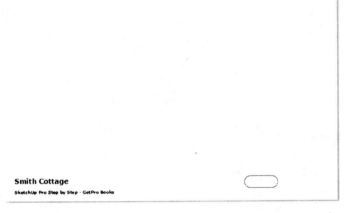

fig. 78

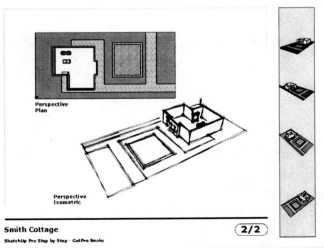

fig. 79

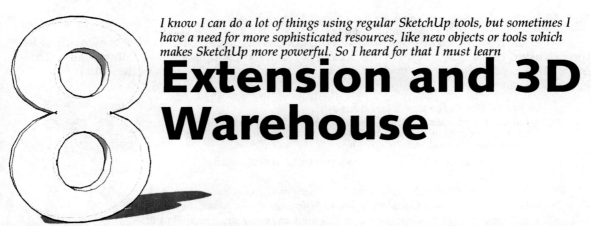

I know I can do a lot of things using regular SketchUp tools, but sometimes I have a need for more sophisticated resources, like new objects or tools which makes SketchUp more powerful. So I heard for that I must learn

Extension and 3D Warehouse

You can increase the possibilities of your work using these extension and 3D warehouse. In this chapter you'll learn how to quickly search and download tools for SketchUp, using Extensions Warehouse, as well as how to download objects and make your projects available in the 3D Warehouse.

What you'll read in this chapter

8.1 Why and how to use Extension Warehouse

8.2 How to import an object from the 3D Warehouse

8.3 How to publish an object to the 3D Warehouse

8.1 Why and how to use Extension Warehouse

Following the trend of many other software manufacturers, SketchUp now has its own app store, the Extension Warehouse. Now it's much easier to look for an application and download it. The installation takes place automatically (in most cases) and the management of these tools has evolved considerably.

to get to the Extension Warehouse

1. On the **Warehouse** toolbar, choose **Extension Warehouse** (you can also use a browser to enter the Extension Warehouse, typing http://www.extensions.sketchup.com).

2. The Extension Warehouse window opens, and you can start exploring:

    a. These are the usual **Back**, **Next** and **Home** navigation buttons;

    b. You have to use a Google account to **Sign In** and download the extensions;

    c. Type a string and click the loupe to search any extensions related to it;

    d. Click this button to **Browse all of the Extensions** listed on the warehouse;

    e. Choose a link from this area to go to the related list of extensions available, based on Categories Industries;

    f. This box shows the **Top Extensions** (most downloaded) for **All Industries**, or the one you select on the bar;

    g. This box shows the **Top Developers**, which are the people that contributes the most for the Extension Warehouse;

    h. If you want to know how to develop and distribute extensions on Extension Manager, click on this link to have all the information about it.

how to download an add-on

The process of downloading an add-on may vary from distributor, but most of the times things are going to happen the way is described below.

1. After finding the extension you would like to use, click on the **Install** button. If you find **"Get this Extension"** written instead, the installation of the add-on shall not be automatic and the rest of the following steps will have no use.

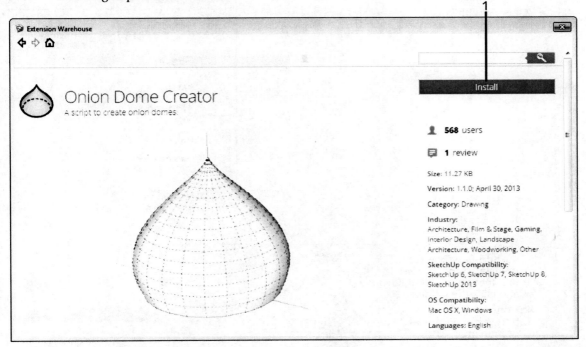

2. Choose **Yes** to let SketchUp download and install this extension for you.

3. Next, you will have to check if the extension was made available as a toolbar (**a**) or as a command under **Window** or **Plugins** menu (**b**).

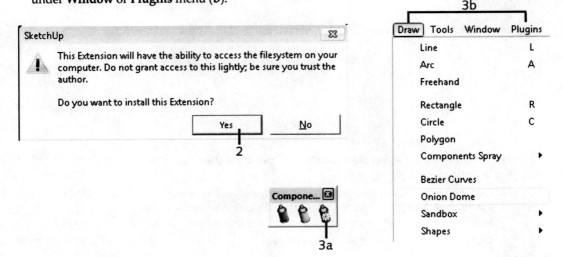

how to uninstall an add-on downloaded from the Extension Warehouse

The Extension Warehouse can easily help you to uninstall add-on; follow these steps:

1. On the **Warehouse** toolbar choose **Extension Warehouse**.
2. Log in with your Google account.

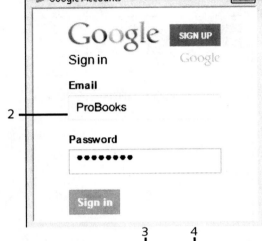

3. Now you have to locate the add-on you want to uninstall; type the name of it into the search field and click the loupe.
4. Notice that the red button has "**Uninstall**" written on it. Click.
5. Follow the next steps, by clicking **Yes**, to have the add-on uninstalled.

how to install an extension that is not on the Extension Warehouse

If you want to install an extension that is not listed on Extension Warehouse, like an add-on that is on Sketchucation forum, you have to download it (must be one or more .rbz files) and follow these steps:

1. On the Window menu, choose **Preferences**.

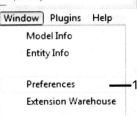

2. Click on
Extensions
(**a**) and then
click on Install
Extension (**b**)....   2a

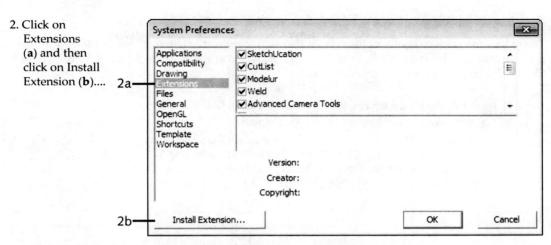

2b

3. Locate the extension (.rbz file) you like to install (**a**) and click **Open** (**b**).

3a

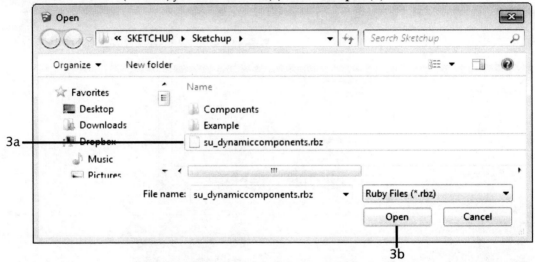

3b

4. Choose **Yes** to let
SketchUp install this
extension for you.

5. Next, you will have to
check if the extension
was made available as
a toolbar or as a menu
command under **Window**
or **Plugins** menu.

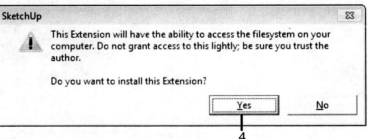

4

NOTE There is no way to remove or uninstall an extension that was not downloaded from the
Extension Warehouse, directly from SketchUp (you have only the option to disable it, in the
Extensions panel). To remove completely this kind of extension from SketchUp, you will have to
locate it in SketchUp/Plugins folder and delete it manually. Better to do this with the SketchUp
closed.

8.2 How to import an object from the 3D Warehouse

There are two ways to get an object from the 3D Warehouse. The first one is for you to import the objects directly to your file, and the other allows you to save the object in a file, separate from SketchUp, to be used in any project later.

how to import an object directly to an active file

1. On the **Warehouse** toolbar, choose **Get Models**.

2. The **Trimble 3D Warehouse** box will appear automatically. Find the object you want to import, typing the name in the indicated field and clicking on **Search** (a). Once you find it, you'll see a button marked **Download Model**. Click on it (b).

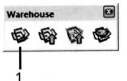

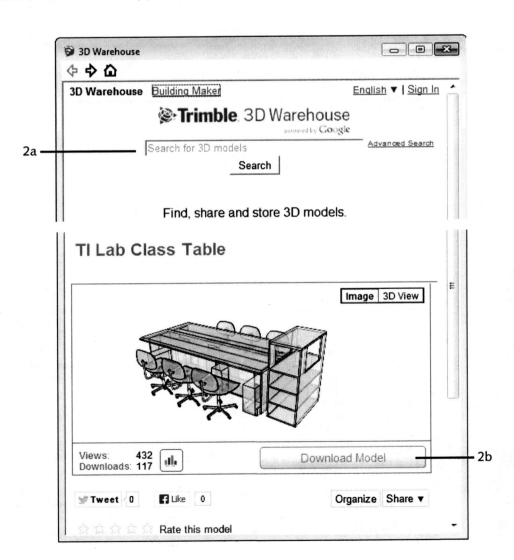

SketchUp Pro 2013 step by step

3. A box will open, asking if you want to use the object in your active file. Choose **Yes**.

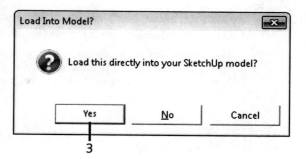

4. Notice how the object is now fixed to the cursor. Click where you want to place the object.

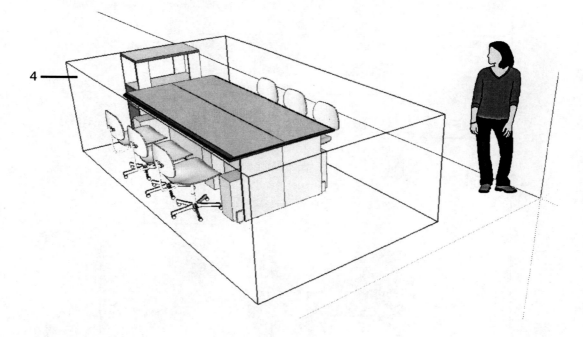

how to get an object from the 3D Warehouse, as an independent file

1. On the **Warehouse** toolbar, choose **Get Models**.

2. The 3D Warehouse window will automatically appear. Find the object you want to import by typing the name in the indicated field and clicking on **Search** (**a**). Once you find it, you'll see a button marked **Download Model**. Click on it (**b**).

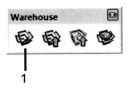

1

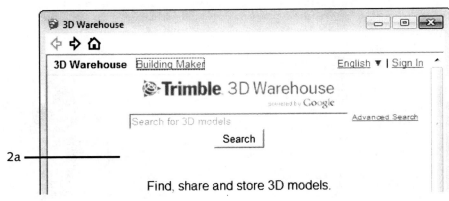

2a

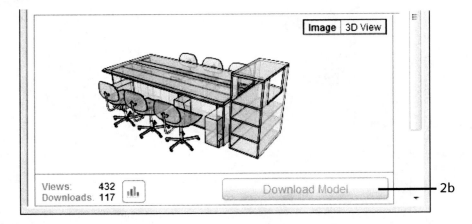

2b

3

3. A box will open, asking whether you want to use the object in your active file. Choose **No**.

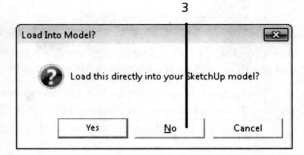

4

4. Another box may open, asking if you want to open the file or only save it. Click on **Save**.

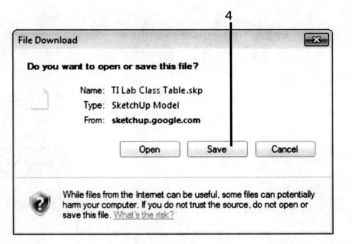

5. Choose the folder in which the file will be saved (**a**), and enter the name (**b**).

6. Click on **Save** to finish the process.

5a

5b

6

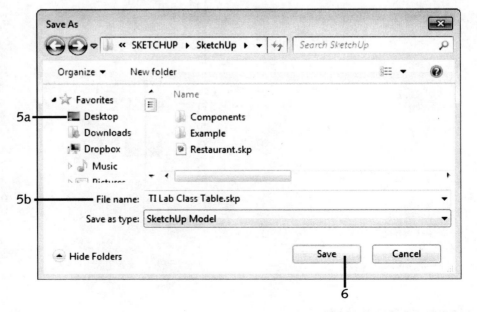

8.3 How to publish an object to the 3D Warehouse

Any object that you've created in SketchUp can be published to the 3D Warehouse where anyone can use it. However, it's necessary for you to have, or create, a Google account in order to do that.

to publish an object to the 3D Warehouse

1. Select the object you want to publish to the 3D Warehouse.

2. On the **Warehouse** toolbar, choose **Share Model**.

3. A box will open, asking you to enter your name (**a**) and password (**b**) for your **Google** account. Enter them, and then choose **Sign in** (**c**). If you don't have an account, click on **SING UP** (**d**).

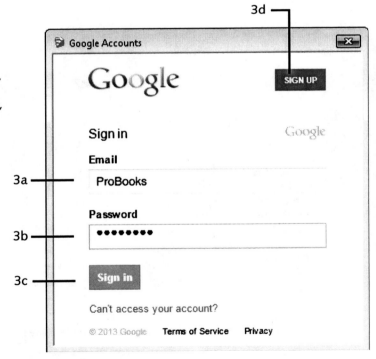

4. Fill in the information about your object:

   a. **Insert model title:** Choose a title for your object;

   b. **Insert model description:** Describe your object;

   c. **Tags:** In this field you can write a list of keywords to be used by the 3D Warehouse to facilitate locating your model for other users;

   d. **Additional content:** Click on the indicated symbol to adjust more items on the object.

5. Click on **Upload**.

6. Notice that a new window is opened with your model, already published. From now on, any 3D Warehouse user can download and use your model.

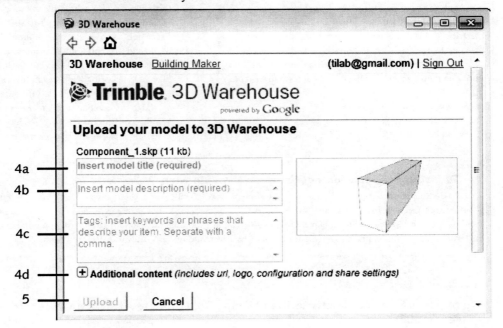

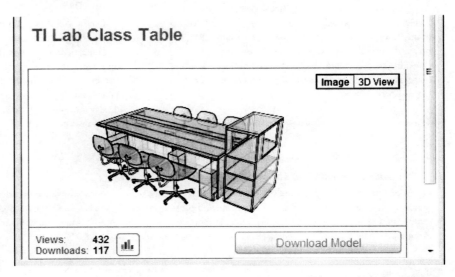

Chapter highlights

To get to the Extension Warehouse (p. 198)

On the **Warehouse** toolbar, choose **Extension Warehouse**. The **Extension Warehouse** window opens, and you can start exploring. You have to use a Google account to sign in and download the extensions. Type a string and click the loupe to search any extensions related to it. If you want to know how to develop and distribute extensions on Extension Manager, must click on "**Develop Center**" and have all the information about it.

How to download an add-on (p. 199)

The process of downloading an add-on may vary from distributor, but most of the times things are going to happen the way is described below. After finding the extension you would like to use, click on the **Install** button. If instead of "**Install**" you find "**Get this Extension**" written in the red button, the installation of the add-on shall not be automatic and the rest of the following steps will have no use. Choose **Yes** to let SketchUp download and install this extension for you. Next, you will have to check if the extension was made available as a toolbar or as a menu command under **Window** or **Plugins** menu.

To install an extension not listed on the Extension Warehouse (p. 200)

To do this, you have to download it (must be one or more .rbz files) and follow these steps. On the **Window** menu, choose **Preferences**. Click on **Extensions** and then click on **Install Extension....** Locate the extension (.rbz file) you like to install and click **Open**. Choose **Yes** to let SketchUp download and install this extension for you. Next, you will have to check if the extension was made available as a toolbar or as a menu command under **Window** or **Plugins** menu.

Import an object directly to the active file (p. 202)

On the **Warehouse** toolbar, choose **Get Models**; locate the object you want to import. Once you find it, you will see a button marked, **Download Model**. Click on it. A box will open, asking if you want to use the object in your active file. Choose **Yes** and notice how the object is now fixed to the cursor. Click where you want to position the object.

How to get an object from the 3D Warehouse as an independent file (p. 204)

On the **Warehouse** toolbar, choose **Get Models**; find the object you want to import. Once you find it, you'll see a button marked, **Download Model**. Click on it. A window will open, asking if you want to use the object in your active file. Choose **No**; another window may open, asking if you want to open the file or save it. Click on **Save** and select a folder where the file will be saved; Click on **Save** to finish the process.

To publish an object to the 3D Warehouse (p. 206)

Select the object that you want to publish to the 3D Warehouse; on the **Warehouse** toolbar, choose **Share Model**. A window will open, asking for your Google name and password. If you don't have an account, click on **Sign up**. Enter the information about your object. Choose **Upload** and notice how a new window is opened, with your model, already published. From this moment, any 3D Warehouse user can download and use your model.

Suggested activities

Ex. 01 – Download an Extension Warehouse add-on

1. You can use any SketchUp file to do these steps.

2. Choose the **Warehouse/Extension Warehouse** and sign in with your Google account.

3. Click on **Drawing** category (*fig. 83*).

4. Scroll down the page until you find the **Onion Dome Creator** add-on. Click on it (*fig. 84*).

fig. 83

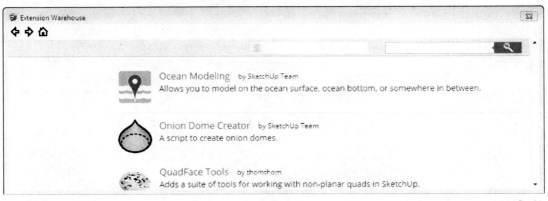

fig. 84

5. Click on **Install** (*fig. 85*) and follow the steps to finish the installation.

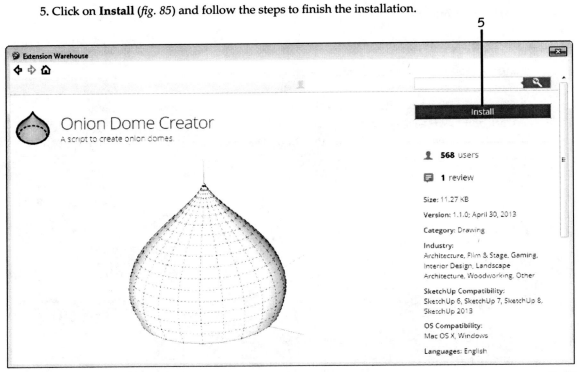

fig. 85

6. Check if the **Onion Dome** was installed on **Draw** menu (*fig. 86*).
   Try to use the add-on to see if works properly.

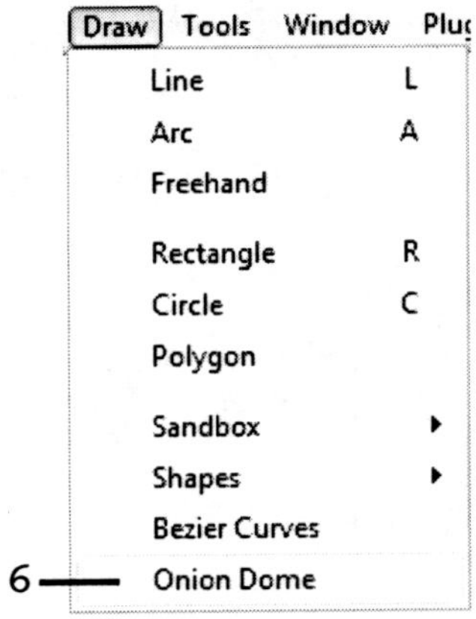

fig. 86

Ex. 02 – Import an object from 3D Warehouse

1. Open the file, **Cap08_Ex02.skp.**

2. Choose **Warehouse/Get Models...** and find the model titled **TI Lab Class Table** (*fig. 87* and *fig. 88*).

3. Download the table to your file and place it in a place inside the house (*fig. 89*).

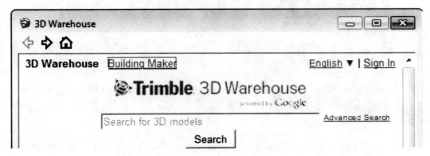

fig. 87

fig. 88

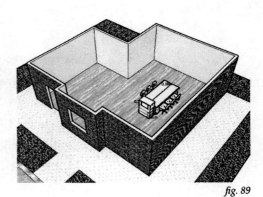

fig. 89

Ex. 03 – Export an object to the 3D Warehouse

1. Open the **Cap08_Ex03.skp** file.

2. Make a few alterations to the **TI Lab Class Table** (*fig. 90*).

3. Choose **Warehouse/Share Model** to publish your table to the 3D Warehouse.

fig. 90

Now that the project is ready, I want to place it on Google Earth, send images to my clients and partners, and I also need to create the executive drawings. I need to know how SketchUp can be used to

interact with Google Earth and other softwares

SketchUp Pro is one of the most communicative computer design softwares that exist. It's possible to see your model in Google Earth, import and export 3D Studio Max and Auto CAD files directly from the SketchUp Pro menu; there are export and import plugins for Revit, Vectorworks, ArchiCAD, Artlantis, and more.

What you'll read in this chapter

9.1 How to see your project on Google Earth

9.2 Importing and exporting images

9.3 Importing and exporting DWG files

9.4 SketchUp and other softwares

9.1 How to see your project on Google Earth

If you used a real world location to create your project on SketchUp (see page **23, to choose a location for your project**), it's time to learn how to export it to Google Earth.

to export and open the project directly on Google Earth

1. Select the project or part of the project to be exported.
2. On the **Google** toolbar, choose **Preview Model in Google Earth**.
3. Notice that Google Earth is automatically opened and your model appears, listed in the window **Places/Temporary Places**, normally under the name **SUPreview**.
4. To confirm that you want to keep your project on Google Earth, click on its name and drag it to **My Places**.

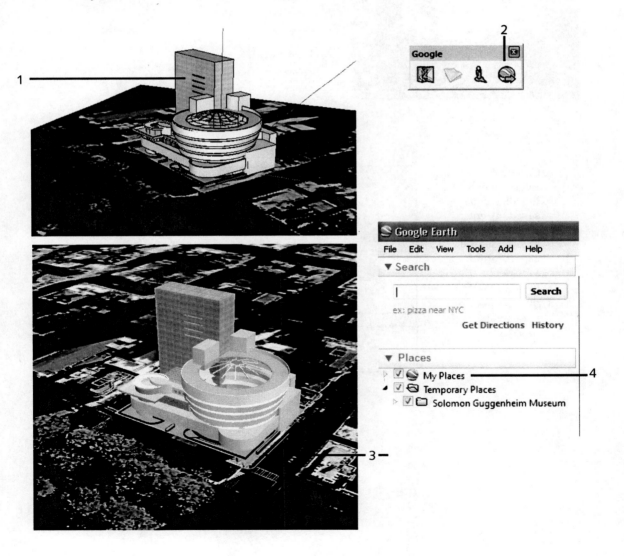

another way to export the project from SketchUp and open in Google Earth

1. Select the project or part of the project to be exported.

2. Choose **File/Export/3D Model....**

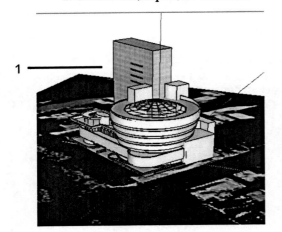

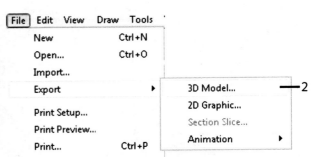

3. Choose the folder where the file will be saved (**a**), enter a name (**b**), and choose the export format for Google Earth (.kmz) (**c**).

4. Click on **Export** to finish the process in SketchUp.

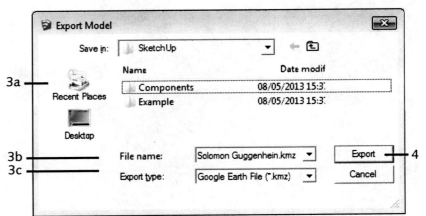

5. In Google Earth, choose **File/Open....**

6. Locate the file.

7. Click on **Open.**

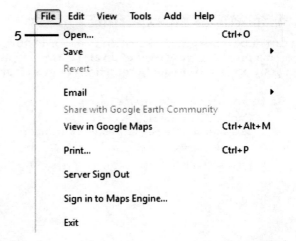

8. Notice that your model appears on the list in the **Places/Temporary Places** window, normally named, **SUPreview.**

9. To confirm that you want to keep your project on Google Earth, click on its name and drag it to the item, **My Places.**

9.2 Importing and exporting images

You can import images in SketchUp to use as textures, painting objects, or as an image to draw over. This process is very easy to do and extremely important because it allows you to use images from your project to create presentations or even make final drawings in other softwares.

to import a single image

1. Choose **File/Import....**
2. Select the image file that you want to import.
3. Choose **Use as image**.
4. Click on **Open**.

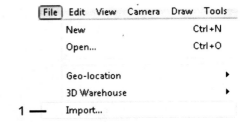

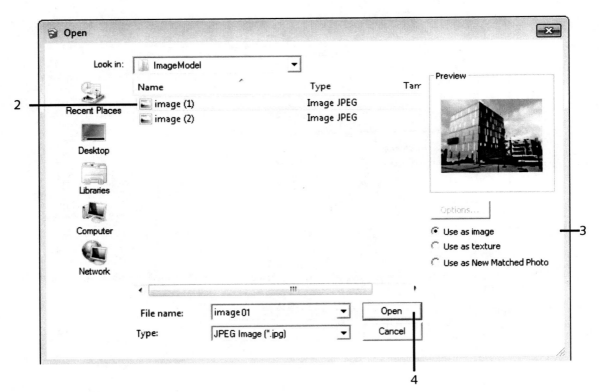

NOTE 1 To use an image as a material, see page **91**.

NOTE 2 To learn how to create objects with the aid of an image, see page **104**.

to export an image

1. Place the viewer in the desired position. Adjust the point of view (with or without a vanishing point), shadows, textures, axes, enable or disable layers, section planes and hidden objects, to make the image how you want it.

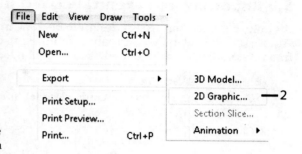

2. Choose **File/Export/2D Graphic....**

3. Enter the name of the file (**a**) and choose the format in the **Save as type** field (**b**). You can choose from the following image formats: JPG, .EPS, .BMP, .TIF, .PNG, and .EPX. You can also export in PDF format.

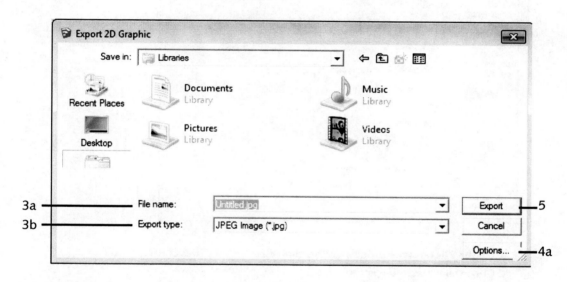

4. To configure image output, click on **Options...** (**a**). Each image format has its own options window. After configuration, click on **OK** (**b**).

5. SketchUp returns to the previous screen. Click on **Export** to finish.

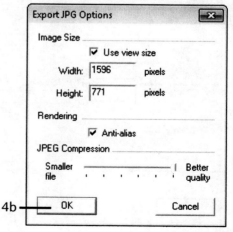

9.3 Importing and exporting DWG files

It's quite common for project design to be done in DWG format, used by softwares such as AutoCAD. SketchUp Pro is capable of importing or exporting your drawings in this format. The free version of SketchUp named SketchUp Make cannot import or export DWG files.

to import a DWG file

1. Configure the units on the **Window/Model Info/Units** menu to the same as the units used in the DWG file.

2. Choose **File/Import....**

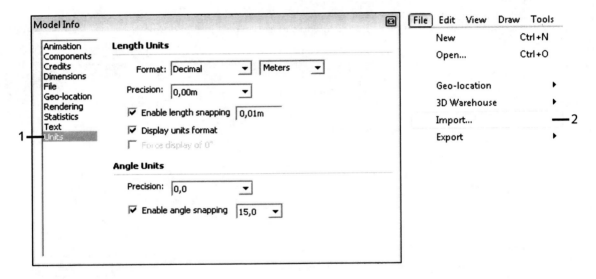

3. On the **Files of type** dropdown list, choose **AutoCAD Files (*.dwg, *.dxf)**.

4. Choose file that you want to import.

5. For import configurations, click on the **Options...** button on the right side of the window.

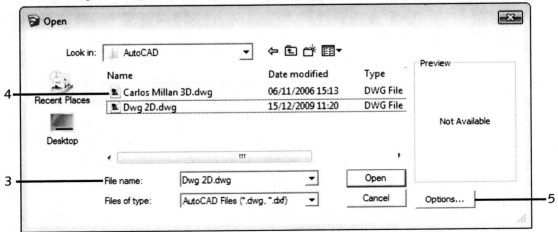

6. Configure these options in the window:

a. **Merge coplanar faces**: Unite, in one face, all those on the same plane;

b. **Orient faces consistently**: Make all external faces with one color and internal faces with another;

c. **Units**: Choose the units used in the origin file;

d. **Preserve drawing origin**: Make SketchUp remember where the drawing origin is.

7. Click on **OK** and notice that SketchUp returns to the previous window.

8. Click on **Open** to finish.

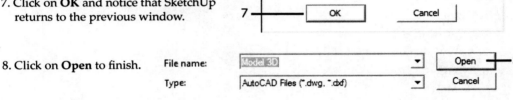

NOTE An imported file comes as a component. To edit, double-click on it. If you prefer to "explode" the object, right-click and choose **Explode**.

---

to export a DWG file

1. Choose **File/Export/2D Graphic...** (to export a 2D drawing) or **File/Export/3D Model...** (to export a 3D object).

2. Type the name of the file (**a**) and choose its format in the field, **Export type** (**b**).

3. For export configuration, click on the **Options...** button, in the lower right corner of the window. After configuring the options, click on **OK**.

4. SketchUp returns to the previous window. Click on **Export** to finish.

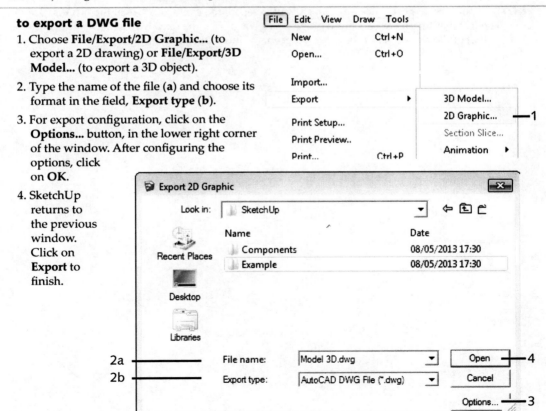

9.4 SketchUp and other softwares

SketchUp Pro is one of the softwares that interacts the most with others. The reason for this good relationship is no CAD program works (until now) like it does. In order for this interaction to work well a series of plugins exist (components installed inside the original program), specifically for each program. These allow the export and import of drawings beyond the formats already existing in the import/export commands in SketchUp Pro itself.

which softwares communicate with SketchUp through plugins?

1. Revit.

2. ArchiCAD.

3. Vectorworks.

4. GIS softwares (SHP format).

5. Artlantis Render and Studio.

6. ArcGIS.

7. 3D Max.

8. Softimage.

> **NOTE** Import and export processes don't always keep all the characteristics of the original drawing. The installation process for these plugins may vary. Visit the SketchUp site (*www.sketchup.com*) and/ or that of the developer of the other program for more information.

Chapter highlights

Export and open the project directly in Google Earth (p. 213)

Select the project or part of the project to be exported; on the **Google** toolbar, choose **Preview Model in Google Earth**.

Google Earth is opened and your model appears, listed in the **Places/Temporary Places** window under the name of **SUPreview**; to keep your project in Google Earth, click on its name and drag it to the item, **My Places**.

Export the SketchUp model and open in Google Earth (p. 214)

Select the project or part of it to be exported and Choose **File/Export/3D Model...**; in the window that opens, choose the folder where the file will be saved, give it a name, and choose the format, **Google Earth** (.kmz); click on **Save** to finish the process in SketchUp. On Google Earth, choose **File/Open** and select the file; notice how your model appears in the list in the window, **Places/Temporary Places**, usually under the name of **SUPreview**; to keep your project in Google Earth, click on its name and drag it to the item, **My Places**.

Importing and exporting images

To import a single image (p. 216)

Choose **File/Import**. In the box that opens, choose the image file (JPG, BMP, TIF, etc.) desired; in that same window, click on the **Use as image** button in the lower right corner. Click on **Open**.

To export an image (p. 217)

Place the viewer in the desired position. Choose **File/Export 2D Graphic...**.

Enter the file name and choose a format in the **Files of type** field. You can choose from the following image formats: JPG, .EPS, .BMP, .TIF, .PNG, .EPX. You can also export in .PDF format. To configure the image output, click on the **Options...** button. After setting the options, click on **OK**; SketchUp returns to the previous window. Click on **OK** to finish.

Importing and exporting DWG files

To import a DWG file (p. 218)

Configure the units in **Window/Model Info/Units**, the same as the units in the DWG file. Choose **File/Import** menu option and in the window **Files of type**, choose ACAD files (*.dwg, *.dxf); select the file you want to import and click on **OK** to finish.

To export a DWG file (p. 219)

Choose **File/Export/2D Graphic...** (to export the drawing in 2D) or **File/Export/3D Model...** (to export the 3D object) enter the name of the file and choose its format in the field, **Export Type**; click on **OK** to finish.

Which softwares interact with SketchUp Pro? (p. 220)

Collada, Revit, ArchiCAD, Vectorworks, Artlantis, ArcGIS, 3D Max, Softimage, formats OBJ, SHP and WRL.

Suggested activities

Ex. 01 – Draw and export a model to Google Earth

1. Open the file **Cap08_Ex01.skp**.

2. Use the **Geo-Location** panel to find the location, "**Metlife Building, New York**" (*fig. 80*).

3. Make a project on the terrain surrounding Metlife Building (*fig. 81*).

4. Select your entire project and choose **Google/Preview Model in Google Earth**.

5. Save your project on Google Earth (*fig. 82*).

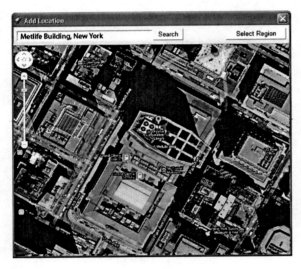

fig. 80

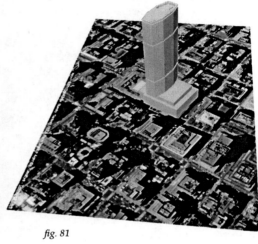

fig. 81

fig. 82

Ex. 02 – Import a .dwg file

1. Open the file **Cap09_Ex01.skp**.

2. Choose **File/Import...** to import the file **Cap09_Ex01.dwg** (*fig. 87*).

3. Use the **Line** and **Rectangle** tools to create surfaces from the lines that came in the DWG file (*fig. 88*).

4. Edit some of the components in the file and notice how the changes made to them are repeated in the other components with the same name (*fig. 89*).

5. After creating the surfaces, use the **Push/Pull** tool to raise the walls (*fig. 90*).

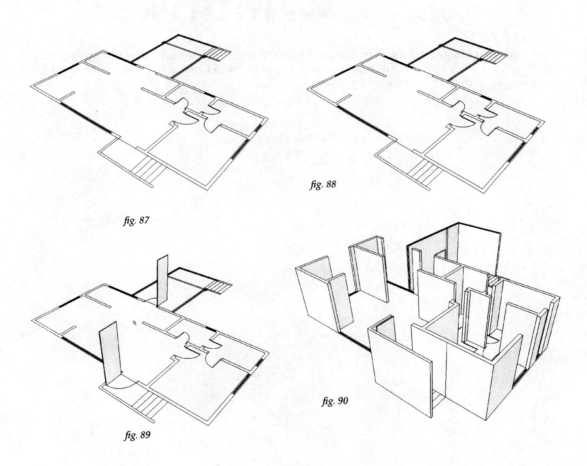

fig. 87

fig. 88

fig. 89

fig. 90

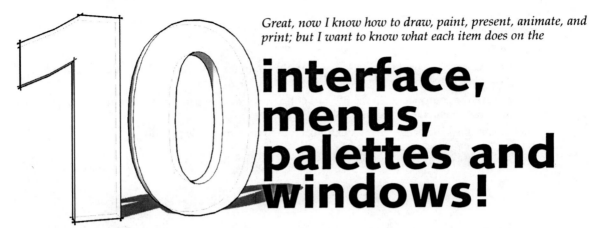

Great, now I know how to draw, paint, present, animate, and print; but I want to know what each item does on the

interface, menus, palettes and windows!

In the following pages, all the commands, tools, settings, and preferences of the program are explained. This book was written based on the version of SketchUp for Windows. On the Mac operating system, some items may vary.

What you'll read in this chapter

10.1 The interface

10.2 Menus

10.3 Palettes

10.4 Window menu

10.5 Model Info menu

10.6 Preferences menu

10.1 The interface

These are the main elements of the SketchUp interface.

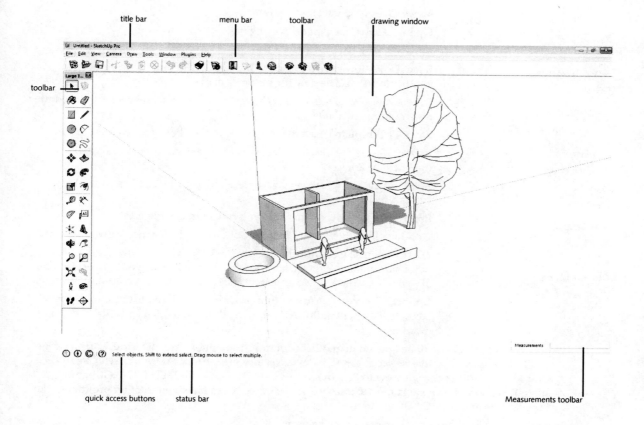

10.2 Menus

New	Ctrl+N
Open...	Ctrl+O
Save	Ctrl+S
Save As...	
Save A Copy As...	
Save As Template...	
Revert	
Send to LayOut	
Preview in Google Earth	
Geo-location	▸
3D Warehouse	▸
Import...	
Export	▸
Print Setup...	
Print Preview...	
Print...	Ctrl+P
Generate Report...	
Recent File	
Exit	

File

New (Ctrl+N): Create a new file.

Open... (Ctrl+O): Open an existing file.

Save (Ctrl+S): Save an active file.

Save As... Allow saving an active file with a different name, or even in another location. The new file becomes active.

Save A Copy As: Does almost the same as **Save As**, however, the saved file does not remain active.

Save As Template... Save the active file in the SketchUp template folder.

Revert: Revert the file to the last version saved. All previous alterations to the last save are lost.

Send to LayOut: Create a project viewport to be placed in a SketchUp LayOut file.

Preview in Google Earth: Open you model in Google Earth.

Geo-location: Show configuration options for the location of your project.

3D Warehouse: Contains the options: **Get Models**, for downloading objects from the internet, **Share Model**, for publishing your project to the 3D Warehouse site, or a component in 3D Warehouse, if you want to share.

Import...: Import files from other programs and formats to SketchUp Pro. Accepts files from AutoCAD, 3DS, in addition to .JPG, and .GIF files, for example.

Export: Export a drawing to be opened in another program. The options are: **3D Model** (create a file in 3D to be opened in diverse programs like Revit, Vectorworks, AutoCAD, and ArchiCAD), **2D Graphic** (export the current view to files in formats like .DWG, .DXF, .JPG, .PICT, .GIF, among others), **Section Slice** (export the section slice in vector format to be edited in other programs, like Vectorworks and AutoCAD) or **Video**.

Print Setup...: Configures preferences for the printer.

Print Preview...: Opens a window for configuration and viewing how the file will be printed, before the print command.

Print (Ctrl+P)...: Print the active file.

Generate Report...: Export a table with all the text information linked to all the objects (or just those selected) inserted in a project.

Recent File: List that shows up to the ten last opened files, allowing you to easily locate them.

Exit: Close SketchUp.

Undo Explode	lt+Backspace
Redo	Ctrl+Y
Cut	Shift+Delete
Copy	Ctrl+C
Paste	Ctrl+V
Paste In Place	
Delete	Delete
Delete Guides	
Select All	Ctrl+A
Select None	Ctrl+T
Hide	
Unhide	▸
Lock	
Unlock	▸
Make Component...	G
Make Group	
Close Group/Component	
Intersect Faces	▸
Face	▸

Edit

Undo (Ctrl+Z): Undo the last command or tool used.

Redo (Ctrl+Y): Redo the last command or tool used.

Cut (Ctrl+X): Make it so an object, selection of objects, or a group is removed from the drawing and placed in the clipboard.

Copy (Ctrl+C): Make it so an object, selection of objects, or a group is copied from the drawing and placed in the clipboard.

Paste (Ctrl+V): Insert an object, selection of objects, or a group that was placed in the clipboard.

Paste in Place: Insert an object in the same position (or, over) the object previously copied. Only works with groups or components.

Delete: Delete the object, various objects, or groups that are selected.

Delete Guides: Delete all the guides from the drawing.

Select All (Ctrl+A): Select all the objects that belong to the active layers.

Select None (Ctrl+T): Deselect all the objects that belong to the active layers and that were selected.

Hide: Hide one or more selected objects.

Unhide: Make one or more hidden objects reappear. To see hidden objects, Choose **View/Hidden Geometry** menu. Options: **Selected** (show the selected hidden objects), **Last** (show the last hidden object) and **All** (show all the hidden objects of the drawing).

Lock: Lock the modification and editing of one or more selected objects.

Unlock: Unlock the modification and editing of one or more selected objects. Options: **Selected** (unlock the selected objects) and **All** (unlock all the objects).

Make Component: Create a component from one or more selected elements.

Make Group: Create a group from one or more selected elements.

Close Group/Component: Exit the editing of a group or component.

Intersect Faces: Create new faces and lines from the intersection between existing lines and faces.

Options: With Model: Create new faces on the selected objects, using all the faces of the model as a reference; **With Selection:** Create new faces only among the selected objects; **With Context:** Create new faces only among the objects selected inside a group or component.

Toolbars ▸	
Scene Tabs	
Hidden Geometry	
Section Planes	
Section Cuts	
Axes	
Guides	
Shadows	
Fog	
Edge Style ▸	
Face Style ▸	
Component Edit ▸	
Animation ▸	

View

Toolbars: Enable and disable the visibility of the toolbars.

Scene Tabs: Enable and disable the bar for changing scenes (which appears from the moment that the file has more than one scene created).

Hidden Geometry: Show hidden objects with the **Edit/Hide** menu. From there, such objects can be changed to visible from the **Edit/Unhide** menu.

Section Planes: Enable and disable display of the section plane objects.

Section Cuts: Enable and disable section cut effects.

Axes: Enable and disable display of the drawing axes.

Guides: Enable and disable display of guides.

Shadows: Enable and disable display of shadows.

Fog: Enable and disable the display of fog.

Edge Style: Enable and disable display of effects in the lines. The options are: **Edges:** Enable or disable display of the drawing lines; **Back Edges:** Show or hide dashed hidden lines; **Profiles**, **Depth Cue**, and **Extension:** Enable or disable these line display options.

Face Style: Control the presentation method of the faces of objects. Contains the same options as in the **Styles** toolbars.

Component Edit: Control the manner in which the 3D model will be shown while editing a component.

Options: Hide Rest of Model (enable and disable the visibility of the entire project) and **Hide Similar Components** (enable and disable the visibility of other copies of the same component).

Animation: The various commands on this menu allow for creating and editing animations of your 3D Model. Options: **Add Scene** (create a scene from the current view), **Update Scene** (update the active scene from the current view), **Delete Scene** (delete the active scene), **Previous Scene** (choose previous scene), **Next Scene** (choose next scene), **Play** (start the animation) and **Settings** (open the control panel for animation time).

Camera

Previous	
Next	
Standard Views	▶
Parallel Projection	
Perspective	
Two-Point Perspective	
Match New Photo...	
Edit Matched Photo	▶
Orbit	O
Pan	H
Zoom	Z
Field of View	
Zoom Window	Ctrl+Shift+W
Zoom Extents	Ctrl+Shift+E
Zoom to Photo	
Position Camera	
Walk	
Look Around	
Image Igloo	I

Previous: Undo the last camera movement.

Next: Redo the last camera movement that was undone.

Standard Views: Show the default views of the program: **Top**, **Bottom**, **Front**, **Back**, **Left**, **Right**, and **Isometric**.

Parallel Projection: Enable the projection of parallel view, without a vanishing point.

Perspective: Enable the projection of perspective view with three vanishing points.

Two-Point Perspective: Enable the projection of perspective view with two vanishing points.

Match New Photo...: Insert an image for execution of photo insertion.

Edit Matched Photo: Open the edit window for the selected matched photo.

Orbit (O): Activate the **Orbit** tool.

Pan (H): Activate the **Panoramic** tool (side move).

Zoom (Z): Activate the **Zoom** tool (zoom in, zoom out).

Field of View: Activate the option for adjusting camera focus.

Zoom Window (Ctrl+Shift+W): Activate the **Zoom Window** tool.

Zoom Extents (Ctrl+Shift+E): Activate the **Center Model** tool.

Zoom to Photo: Zoom in on the matched photo.

Position Camera: Activate the **Position Camera** tool, which allows you to place the viewer in a specific area of the project.

Walk: Activate the **Walk** tool, which allows you to walk through the project.

Look Around: Activate the **Look Around** tool, which changes the screen view without changing places.

Image Igloo (I): Show, all at one time, all the images used as a reference for creating a building with the **Building Maker**.

Draw

Line	L
Arc	A
Freehand	
Rectangle	R
Circle	C
Polygon	
Sandbox	▶

Line (L): Enable the tool for drawing lines.

Arc (A): Enable the tool for building arcs.

Freehand: Enable the tool for drawing freehand.

Rectangle (R): Enable the tool that draws rectangles.

Circle (C): Enable the tool for drawing circles.

Polygon: Enable the tool for building regular polygons.

Sandbox: Show the tools that are used, most times, for creation of terrain.

Select	space
Eraser	E
Paint Bucket	B
Move	M
Rotate	Q
Scale	S
Push/Pull	P
Follow Me	
Offset	F
Outer Shell	
Solid Tools	▶
Tape Measure	T
Protractor	
Axes	
Dimensions	
Text	
3D Text	
Section Plane	
Advanced Camera Tools	▶
Interact	
Sandbox	▶

Tools

Select (Space bar): Activate the **Select** tool.

Eraser (E): Activate the **Eraser**, for deleting lines and faces.

Paint Bucket (B): Activate the **Paint** tool, for painting the faces of objects.

Move (M): Activate the **Move** tool, for moving lines, faces, and entire objects.

Rotate (Q): Activate the **Rotate** tool, for rotating the select elements of the drawing.

Scale (S): Activate the **Scale** tool, for scaling objects.

Push/Pull (P): Activate the **Push/Pull** tool, for creating and altering objects starting from other objects and/or plane surfaces.

Follow Me: Activate the **Follow Me** tool, which creates an object starting from a path and a sequence of lines that function as a path.

Offset (F): Activate the **Offset** tool.

Outer Shell: Remove internal faces and lines from one or more groups or components that overlap.

Solid Tools: Show the tools for operation of solids. Options: **Intersect** (create a new object starting from one or more groups or components that overlap), **Union** (create a single object starting from one or more groups or components that overlap), **Subtract** (create a new object starting from the geometric subtraction of a first selected object and a second selected object), **Trim** (remove the geometry of a first selected object and a second selected object), and **Split** (create new objects from one or more groups or components that overlap, dividing them).

Tape Measure (T): Enable the **Tape Measure** tool, which allows for creating **Guides**.

Protractor: Enable the **Protractor** tool, which creates **Angular Guides**.

Axes: Activate the **Axes** tool, which serves to change the direction of the axes that orient the project.

Dimensions: Activate the **Dimension** tool, which measure distances and create dimension lines.

Text: Enable the **Text** tool, which inserts text notes in the project.

3D Text: Enable the **3D Text** tool, which creates text in 3D.

Section Plane: Activate the **Section Planes** tool, which allows for slicing an object in the project.

Advanced Camera Tools: Shows various tools used to create and manage cameras, entities that are used by the movie industry. Do not confuse with **Scenes**, this type of camera has it's own way to be worked with.

Interact: Activate a pre-programmed action in a dynamic component.

Sandbox: Show the tools that are used, among other things, to create a terrain.

Model Info

Entity Info

Materials

Components

Styles

Layers

Outliner

Scenes

Shadows

Fog

Match Photo

Soften Edges

Instructor

Preferences

Extension Warehouse

Hide Dialogs

Ruby Console

Component Options

Component Attributes

Photo Textures

Window

Model Info: Opens the **Model Info** window, which allows configuration of various parameters used by the program.

Entity Info: The **Entity Info** menu shows the main information of the selected object(s).

Materials: Opens the **Materials** window, which serves to create, edit, and find textures that are applied without the SketchUp objects.

Components: Opens the **Components** window, which manages the use and creation of components.

Styles: Shows the **Styles** window, which saves and controls diverse pre-configurations for the appearance of your drawing.

Layers: Opens the management window for layers.

Outliner: Opens the **Outliner** window, which manages components and groups of the project.

Scenes: Activates the window that manages **Scenes**, which record the display of a project.

Shadows: The **Shadows** window enables, disables, and adjusts shadows themselves, projected by SketchUp.

Fog: Controls the settings for fog, which can be applied to your project.

Match Photo: Enable or disable the **Match Photo** window.

Soften Edges: Opens the window that regulates the smoothness of curved objects.

Instructor: Opens the **Instructor** window, which gives hints about using the program.

Preferences: Opens the configuration window for SketchUp preferences.

Extension Warehouse: Find and download SketchUp add-ons that can improve SketchUp skills.

Hide/Show Dialogs: Hide or show, automatically, all the windows and toolbars.

Ruby Console: Opens the window for programming in **Ruby**.

Component Options: Allows adjustments in dynamic components.

Component Attributes: Allows for complete editing of a dynamic component, including or removing parameters and altering their default measurements.

Photo Textures: Opens the **Photo Textures** window for importing and using images from Google Street View and Panoramio.com as textures.

10.3 Palettes

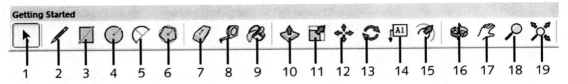

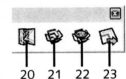

Getting Started

1. **Select:** To select or unselect objects.

2. Draw lines and/or irregular polygons.

3. Draw rectangles.

4. Draw circles.

5. Draw arcs.

6. Draw polygons.

7. **Eraser:** For deleting objects from the drawing.

8. **Tape Measure:** Measures distances and creates guides

9. **Paint Bucket:** For painting faces of objects.

10. **Push/Pull:** Create objects from faces.

11. **Scale:** Scale edges, faces, or whole objects.

12. **Move:** Move and/or copy lines, faces, or whole objects.

13. **Rotate:** Rotate lines, faces, or whole objects.

14. **Text:** Insert a text notation in the project.

15. **Offset:** Create lines parallel to others previously selected. These lines need to make a face.

16. **Orbit:** Make the viewer orbit (spin in all directions) around the center of the axes of orientation. You can activate **Orbit** by pressing and holding the click wheel.

17. **Pan:** Laterally move the viewer in relation to the project. You can activate **Pan** by pressing and holding the click wheel together with the left button.

18. **Zoom:** Zoom in or out with the viewer on the center of the screen. Press the **Shift** key and drag the cursor up and down to adjust the focal distance.

19. **Zoom Extents:** Create a view that shows all the objects drawn, all at one time on the screen.

20. **Add Location:** Opens a window for you to choose the location of your project.

21. **Get Models...:** Find and download SketchUp models that are in the 3D Warehouse.

22. **Extension Warehouse:** Find and download SketchUp add-ons that can improve SketchUp skills.

23. **Send to Layout:** Send the active document to SketchUp Layout.

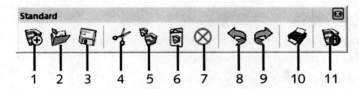

Standard

1. Create a new file.

2. Open an existing file.

3. Save an active file.

4. Cut the selection for the transfer area.

5. Copy the selection to the transfer area.

6. Paste the selection.

7. Delete the selected object(s).

8. Undo the last action.

9. Redo the last action undone.

10. Print the project in the current view.

11. Open the **Model Info** window.

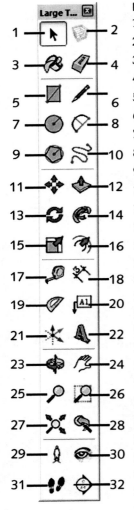

Large Tool Set

1. **Select:** For selecting and unselecting objects.

2. **Component Maker:** Transform the selected drawing(s) into component(s).

3. **Paint Bucket:** For painting faces of objects.

4. **Eraser:** For deleting objects from the drawing.

5. Draw rectangles.

6. Draw lines and/or irregular polygons.

7. Draw circles.

8. Draw arcs.

9. Draw regular polygons.

10. Draw freehand.

11. **Move:** Move and/or copy lines, faces, or objects.

12. **Push/Pull:** Create objects from faces.

13. **Rotate:** Rotate lines, faces, or whole objects.

14. **Follow Me:** Create an object from a face of reference and a sequence of lines that form a path.

15. **Scale:** Scale edges, faces, or whole objects.

16. **Offset:** Create lines that are parallel to others previously selected. Such lines need to make a face.

17. **Tape Measure:** Measure distances, create guide lines and points.

18. **Dimension:** Measure distance and create dimension lines.

19. **Protractor:** Measure angles and create angular guide lines.

20. **Text:** Insert a text notation in the project.

21. **Axes:** Change the direction of the axes that orient the project.

22. **3D Text:** Insert a 3D text in the project.

23. **Orbit:** Make the viewer orbit (turn in all directions) around the center of the screen. You can activate the **Orbit** by pressing and holding the click wheel.

24. **Pan:** Move the viewer laterally in relation to the project.

25. **Zoom:** Zoom in or out with the viewer in the center of the screen. Press **Shift** and drag the cursor up or down to adjust the focus.

26. **Zoom Window:** Allows for zooming the viewer like a window; to use, click and drag diagonally, forming a rectangle.

27. **Zoom Extents:** Adjust the view to show all the objects drawn, all at one time on the screen.

28. **Previous:** Return the camera to the previous position.

29. **Position Camera:** Allows you to place the viewer in a specific place in the project.

30. **Look Around:** Change the point of view of the viewer, without moving out of place.

31. **Walk:** Allows you to stroll through the project.

32. **Section Plane:** Slice an object in the project.

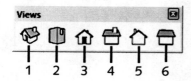

Views

1. Isometric view.
2. Top view.
3. Front view.
4. Right view.
5. Rear view.
6. Left view.

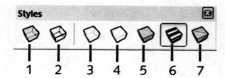

Styles

1. Enable and disable **X-Ray** mode.
2. Enable and disable **Back Edges** mode, which shows and hides dashed hidden lines.
3. Activate **Wireframe** display.
4. Display the project in **Hidden Line** mode.
5. Place in **Shaded** display mode.
6. Enable **Shaded with Textures** mode.
7. Enable **Monochrome** mode.

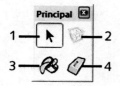

Principal

1. **Select:** For selecting and deselecting objects.
2. **Component Maker:** Transform selected object(s) into component(s).
3. **Paint Bucket:** For painting faces of objects.
4. **Eraser:** For deleting objects from the drawing.

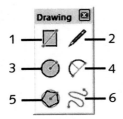

Drawing

1. Draw rectangles.

2. Draw lines and/or irregular polygons.

3. Draw circles.

4. Draw arcs.

5. Draw regular polygons.

6. Draw freehand.

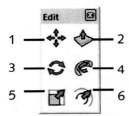

Modification

1. **Move:** Move and/or copy lines, faces, or whole objects.

2. **Push/Pull:** Create objects from faces.

3. **Rotate:** Rotate lines, faces, or whole objects.

4. **Follow Me:** Create an object from a face of reference and a sequence of lines that form a path.

5. **Scale:** Scale lines, faces, or whole objects.

6. **Offset:** Create lines that are parallel to others previously selected. Such lines need to make a face.

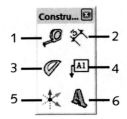

Construction

1. **Tape Measure:** Measure distance and create guides.

2. **Dimensions:** Measure distance and create dimension lines.

3. **Protractor:** Measure angles and create guides from them.

4. **Text:** Insert a text notation in the project.

5. **Axes:** Position and align axes that orient the drawing.

6. **3D Text:** Insert a 3D text in the project.

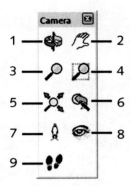

Camera

1. **Orbit**: Make the viewer orbit (turn in all directions) around the center of the axes of orientation.

2. **Pan**: Laterally move the viewer in relation to the project.

3. **Zoom**: Zoom the viewer in or out. Press **Shift** and drag the cursor up or down to adjust the focal distance.

4. **Zoom Window**: Allows for zooming the viewer like a window; to use, click and drag diagonally, forming a rectangle.

5. **Zoom Extents**: Create a view that shows all the objects draw, all at one time on the screen.

6. **Previous**: Return the camera to the previous position.

7. **Position Camera**: Allows you to place the viewer in a specific place in the project.

8. **Walk**: Allows you to stroll through the project.

9. **Look Around**: Change the point of view of the viewer without moving it out of place.

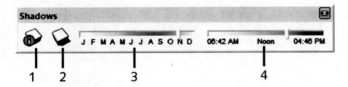

Shadows

1. Open the **Window/Shadows** menu.

2. Enable or disable shadows in the project.

3. Dropdown list for choosing the date of viewing shadows in the project.

4. Dropdown list for choosing the hour of viewing shadows.

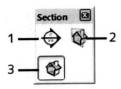

Section Planes

1. **Section Planes:** Slice an object in the project.

2. Show or hide the section plane.

3. Show or hide the object sliced by a section plane.

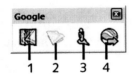

Google

1. **Add Location:** Open a window for choosing the location of your project.

2. **Toggle Terrain:** Alternate the view of the Google Earth image between 2D and 3D.

3. **Photo Textures:** Open the **Photo Textures** window for importing and using Google Street View and Panoramio.com images as textures.

4. **Preview Model in Google Earth:** Export your project in the format of Google Earth.

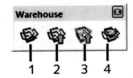

Warehouse

1. **Get Models...:** Search and download SketchUp models that are in the 3D Warehouse.

2. **Share Model...:** Send your SketchUp model to be shared via the 3D Warehouse.

3. **Share Component...:** Select a component and click this button to share it in the 3D Warehouse.

4. **Extension Warehouse:** Takes you to the Extension Warehouse, a site to find and easily install add-ons for SketchUp.

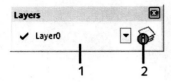

Layers
1. Choose the active layer.
2. Open the **Layers** window.

Dynamic Components
1. **Interact with dynamic components**: Activate a pre-programmed action in a dynamic component.
2. **Component Options**: Open the window that alters the settings of the selected dynamic component.
3. **Component Attributes**: Open the window that alters the programming of the selected dynamic component.

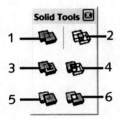

Solid Tools
1. **Outer Shell**: Remove internal lines and faces from one or more groups or components that overlap. These objects can be preselected or be selected after clicking the button.
2. **Intersect**: Create a new object from one or more groups or components that overlap. These objects can be preselected or be selected after clicking the button.
3. **Union**: Create a single object from one or more groups or components that overlap. These objects can be preselected or be selected after clicking the button.
4. **Subtract**: Create a new object from the subtracted geometry of a first selected object and a second selected object. The first selected object will disappear. The objects should be groups or components.
5. **Trim**: Remove the geometry of a first selected object in a second selected object. The first selected object remains. The objects should be groups or components.
6. **Split**: Create new objects from one or more groups or components that overlap, dividing them. These objects can be preselected or be selected after clicking the button.

10.4 Window Menu

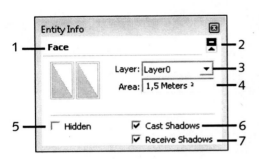

Entity Info

1. Name of the selected object.

2. Show or hide more options for the selected object.

3. **Layer:** Show which layer the object is associated with.

4. Fields with information that varies according to the object(s) selected are shown in this area.

5. **Hidden:** Hide or show the selected object.

6. **Cast Shadows:** Make the object project its shadow on others, when that is the case.

7. **Receive Shadows:** Make the object received shade from others, when that is the case.

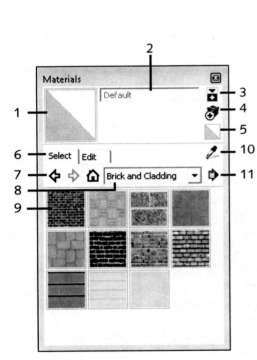

Materials-Select

1. Show the image of the material in use.

2. Show the name of the material in use.

3. Show or hide the secondary selection pane.

4. Create a new material.

5. Make the SketchUp default material active.

6. Toggle between **Select** mode, for selecting the material to be used, and **Edit** mode, for editing the selected material (only functions when the active material belongs to the project in use).

7. **Previous** (return to a library, during search), and **Next** (advance to a library), and **In Model** (show the library from the active file) buttons.

8. Choose the library to be shown in the smaller window, for choosing the material to be used.

9. Show the materials from the library chosen in **8**.

10. Activate sample paint, for making a material that is applied to a face in the project active.

11. Open various options for managing materials.

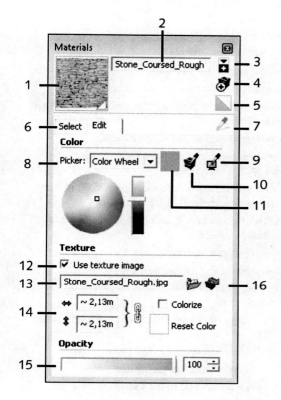

Materials-Edit (Windows version)

1. Show the image of the material in use.

2. Show the name of the material in use.

3. Show or hide the secondary selection pane.

4. Create a new material.

5. Activate the SketchUp default material.

6. Toggle between **Select** mode, for selecting the material to be used, and **Edit** mode, for editing the selected material (only functions when the active material belongs to the project in use).

7. Sample paint, for choosing the prime materials that are applied in the project.

8. Toggle between the methods for selecting colors that make a material.

9. Sample paint for choosing only the color of a material existing in a library (without opacity or texture information, for example).

10. Sample paint for choosing only the color of a material applied to an object in the project (without opacity or texture information, for example).

11. Undo all the color alterations.

12. Enable and disable the use of an image file (defined in **13**) for making a material.

13. Allows you to choose an image file for making a material.

14. Set the real size of an image in the project.

15. Set the degree of opacity of the color chosen.

16. Open the program for editing images (defined in **Window/Preferences**).

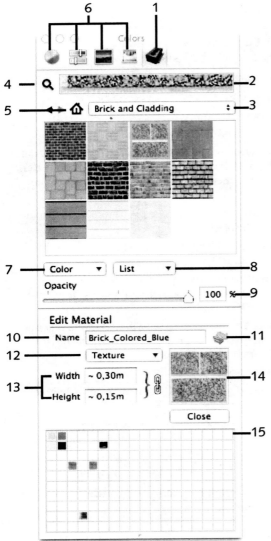

Materials-Edit (Mac version)

1. Shows the texture pallete

2. Show the image of the material in use.

3. Choose a material library from this dropdown list.

4. Sample paint, for choosing the prime materials that are applied in the project.

5. Shows all the materials used in the model.

6. Toggle between the methods for selecting colors that can be mixed with a material.

7. Click to view the texture edition options: **Edit, remove, duplicate** and **new texture**.

8. Click to view the lists configurations: **New, duplicate, remove** and **purge unused**.

9. Set the opacity of the material.

10. Show the name of the material in use.

11. Open the program for editing images (defined in **Window/Preferences**).

12. Allows to change or remove the texture file and reset the color.

13. Set the real size of an image in the project.

14. Show the image of the material in use.

15. Click and drag a material to the favorites area.

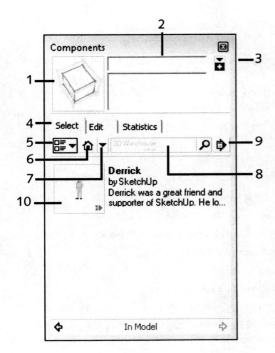

Components

1. Show the image of the selected component.

2. Show the name of the selected component.

3. Show or hide the secondary selection pane.

4. Toggle between **Select** mode, for selecting the component, **Edit**, for editing the selected component (only available when the active material belongs to the project in use), and **Statistics**, which gives technical information about the elements that make up the selected component.

5. Click this button to choose the mode in which to view objects, in the window described in **10**.

6. Click this button to see the components that are in the library in your file.

7. Click to gain access to the components in your favorites folders and from recently used files.

8. Search box for components on 3D Warehouse.

9. Shows various options for managing the libraries.

10. Shows the components that are stored in the active file.

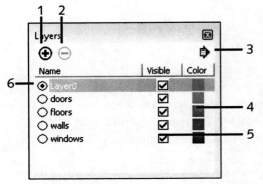

Layers

1. **Add:** Add a layer to the active file.

2. **Delete:** Delete the selected layer in the list below.

3. Show other options for management of the layers.

a. **Select All:** Select all the layers;
b. **Purge:** Delete the layers that are not used;
c. **Color by layer:** Paint the objects according to the color of the layer.

4. Double-click the square to set the color of the layer.

5. Show or hide objects from a particular layer.

6. Choose the active layer by clicking the circle.

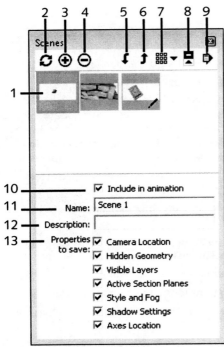

Scenes

1. List of recorded scenes up to the moment. Click on the name of one to activate.

2. **Update:** Update the selected scenes in the list below starting from the current position of the viewer.

3. **Add:** Add a scene to the list, starting from the current position of the viewer.

4. **Delete:** Delete an active scene.

5. Move the scene one position up in the order of scenes.

6. Move the scene one position down.

7. Choose how the scenes appear in the field described in **1**.

8. Show the options of the secondary selection pane.

9. Show other options for managing scenes.

10. Include the active scene in the animation.

11. **Name:** Rename the active scene.

12. **Description:** For placing comments about the active scene.

13. **Properties to save:** Choose which properties of the project will be saved by the active scene.

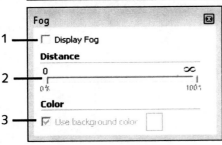

Fog

1. **Display Fog:** Enable or disable the effect of fog.

2. **Distance:** Adjust the distance from where the fog begins and to where it will reach its maximum point.

3. **Color:** Allows you to choose the color of the fog.

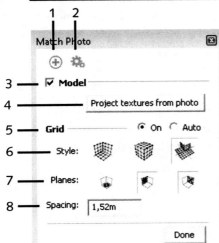

Match Photo

1. Import an image as a matched photo.

2. Allows the editing of an existing matched photo.

3. **Model:** Enable or disable the visibility of the model.

4. **Project textures from photo:** Project the image in the model as if it were a texture.

5. **Grid:** Toggle between **On** (grid always on) and **Auto** (grid only on when a matched photo is used).

6. **Style:** Toggle between the types of grid that match best with the perspective of your image.

7. **Planes:** Enable and disable the grid of each plane.

8. **Spacing:** Adjust the grid scale.

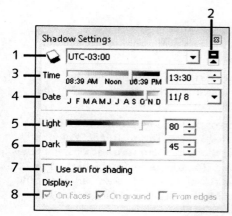

Shadow Settings

1. Click this button to enable or disable the projection of shadows.

2. Show or hide options **5**, **6** and **7**, described just below.

3. **Time:** Choose the house used as a reference for solar illumination.

4. **Date:** Choose the day used as a reference for solar illumination.

5. **Light:** Adjust the quantity of light applied directly on the faces of objects.

6. **Dark:** Adjust the intensity of shadows applied in the project.

7. **Use the sun for shading:** Use the position of the sun to calculate the lighting of object faces, when item **1** is disabled.

8. **Display:** Choose where shadows will be projects: **On faces** (on the faces of objects), **On ground** (on the ground of the project), **From edges** (calculate the shadows of the edges of objects).

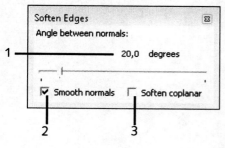

Soften Edges

All the operations involving the **Soften Edges** window need to be done with some line(s) selected.

1. **Angle between normals:** Disable the lines that connect surfaces with angles between them that are smaller than what is set on the bar.

2. **Smooth normals:** Add a light and texture effect to areas where lines were removed.

3. **Soften coplanar:** Enable and disable lines of complex polygons during setting **1**.

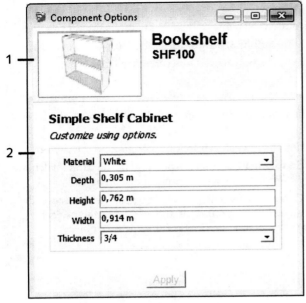

Component Options

This window allows configuration of a dynamic component.

1. In this area, an image of the selected dynamic component appears; to the side, the name of the component is shown.

2. In this part of the window, all the fields that can be adjusted appear. The quantity of fields and allowed alterations for them varies according to the object selected. To insert or remove fields and/or modify their default values, it's necessary to use the **Component Attributes** window (not available for the free version of SketchUp).

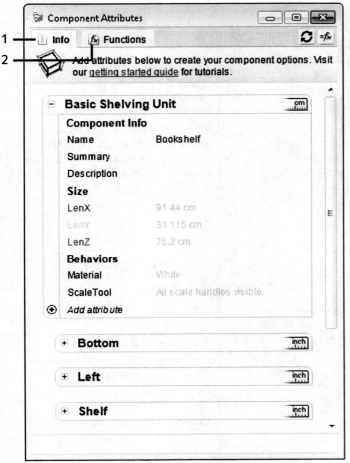

Component Attributes

This window allows you to add, remove, or edit parameters of a dynamic component. You can also use this window to create parameters in a normal component, transforming it into a dynamic component.

1. **Info:** In this area of the window you include, edit, and remove parameters (called attributes) of the dynamic component.

2. **Functions:** On this tab, choose what function will be linked to the particular parameter, and you can also define how this function will be presented to the user.

10.5 Model Info Menu

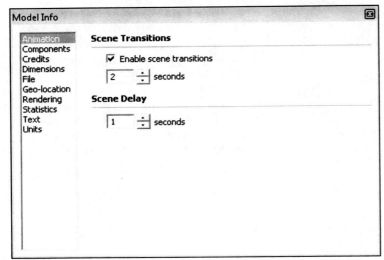

Animation

Scene Transitions: Enables the transitions between scenes and controls the duration of transition between them.

Scene Delay: Adjusts the time SketchUp shows a scene during the execution of an animation.

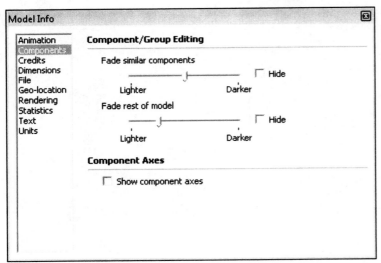

Components

Component/Group Editing: Adjust the way (stronger or weaker) in which SketchUp shows similar components and/or the rest of the model.

Component Axes: Show the axes of creation of the components at the time of editing.

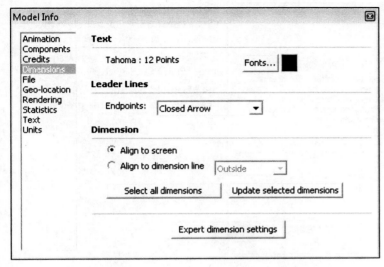

Dimensions

Text: Control the characteristics of the text used for dimension lines.

Leader Lines: Adjust the style of the points of leader lines.

Dimension: Adjust the way the dimension lines will appear in relation to the position of the viewer.

Expert dimension settings: Open a new window with more settings for dimension lines.

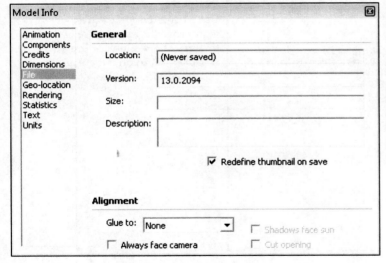

File

General: Shows general information on the file used at the moment.

Alignment: Adjusts the alignment of entry of a component or of a model, imported to the current file (**Glue to**); determine if the component can cut faces (doors in walls, for example, **Cut opening** option) or if it will always facing the active camera (**Always face camera**).

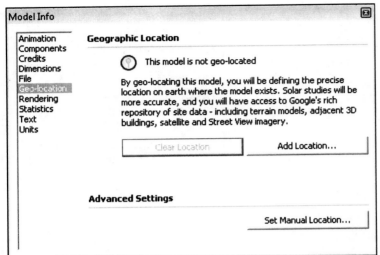

Geo-location

Clear Location: Click to delete the location reference from your file.

Add Location...: Allows choosing the location of the project.

Set Manual Location...: Adjust the position of the sun in the project.

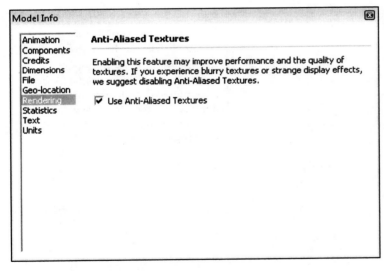

Rendering

Use Anti-Aliased Textures: Click to improve the appearance of the textures applied in your project. Disable this option if there are problems with the display of any textures.

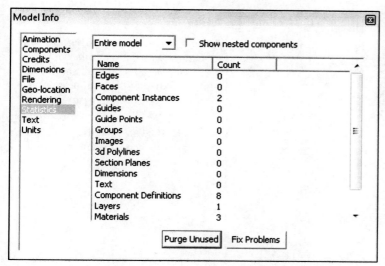

Statistics

This option displays the technical information of all the objects in the model, or by component, and also executes corrective operations in the objects (options **Purge Unused** and **Fix Problems**).

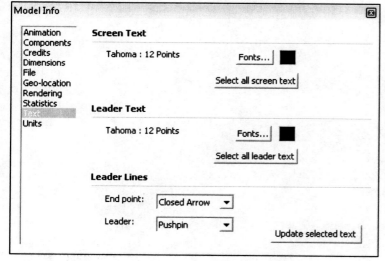

Text

Screen Text: Allows setting the type of text used alone (font, size, color, etc.).

Leader Text: For choosing the type of text used for leader lines on a SketchUp object (font, size, color, etc.).

Leader Lines: Adjust the characteristics of the **Text** tool, from the style of arrows to the style of the line itself.

Update selected text: Use the information in this window to update and modify all the text previously selected.

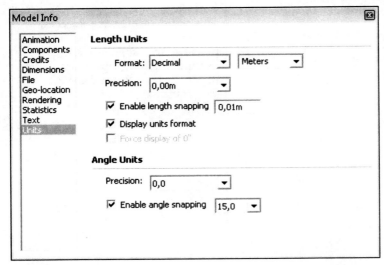

Units

Length Units: Configure the document units, the number of decimal places and length snapping, shown to display the unit mark and dimension objects in the program's information fields.

Angle Units: Establish the precision of angular dimensions and the angle snap value.

10.6 Preferences Menu

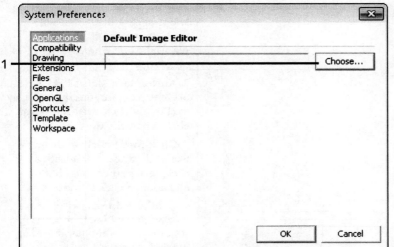

Applications

1. Click on the **Choose...** button to select which image editing program will be used for handling SketchUp textures.

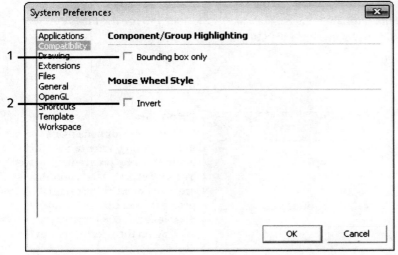

Compatibility

1. The **Bounding box only** option enables the box that limits the selected component, or all the boxes for components that are "above" the selection also.

2. Option that inverts the zoom direction when the click wheel is rolled.

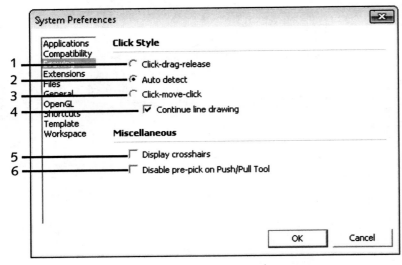

Drawing

1. **Click-drag-release:** In this way, the line is drawn by clicking and dragging the mouse with the button pressed. SketchUp places the line when the button is released.

2. **Auto detect:** Makes it so SketchUp determines the best way to click, by **click-drag-release** or **click-move-click**.

3. **Click-move-click:** In this way, SketchUp draws a line with a click, release the mouse button, and another click to confirm.

4. **Continue line drawing:** Make it so, with the **Line** tool, SketchUp continues with another line after the first is drawn.

5. **Display crosshairs:** Show lines, starting from the cursor position on the screen, that represent the three orientation axes of the drawing.

6. **Disable pre-pick on Push/Pull Tool:** Enable and disable the ability to use the **Push/Pull** tool with a preselected face, clicking on any area of the screen.

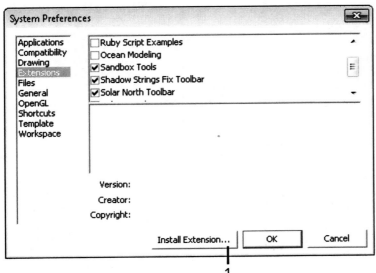

Extensions

1. The various options that appear in this window refer to the tools made by **Ruby** programming, or by the SketchUp team, and that are not present in the original program. You can enable and disable each one of them by clicking on their corresponding boxes.

2. Click on **Install Extension...** to install an add-on (.rbz file) that is not listed on Extension Warehouse.

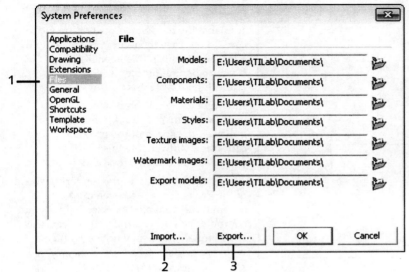

Files

1. The folders containing various types of files necessary for SketchUp to function are listed in these fields. Click on the folder icon beside the type of file to change the location of the respective folder.

2. **Import...**: Import location settings of files previously saved.

3. **Export...**: Export location settings of files that can be used by another SketchUp file.

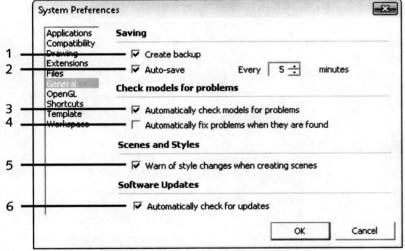

General

1. Click beside **Create backup** for the program to automatically make a backup copy of your work file.

2. Enable **Auto-save**, which automatically saves your work file.

3. If this item is enabled, SketchUp automatically searches for problems while the program is in use. It's a good idea to always leave this on.

4. If this item is enabled, SketchUp will automatically correct all the problems it finds. If it's not, every time there is a problem, SketchUp will interrupt your work to show the error and ask what to do (fix now, fix later, don't fix).

5. With this item enabled, SketchUp will alert you every time you've changed style, before recording a scene.

6. **Automatically check for updates**: Enable and disable the automatic search for SketchUp updates.

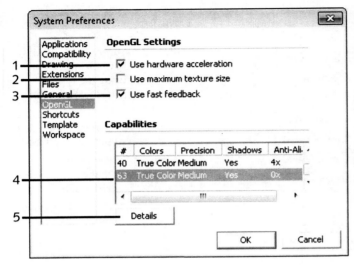

OpenGL

1. Enable the hardware acceleration video card, to increase the rendering speed. Only works well with 100% OpenGL cards. If you're having problems with video rendering, disable this option.

2. If you enable this box, SketchUp will increase the display quality of textures; however, the speed of the program in use can suffer. Only enable this box if your computer has a really good video card.

3. This option increases the rendering speed of the project on screen even more and is automatically enabled by SketchUp if your computer can utilize it. If you activate the box manually, you may notice problems with your video.

4. Table that shows the suggested video configurations for your equipment. You can activate the last option on the table, which is usually the most appropriate.

5. **Details:** Show the technical details of the item selected in **4**.

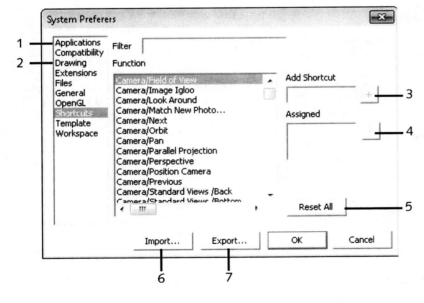

Shortcuts

1. **Filter:** Filter the menu below to improve the search for the desired shortcut.

2. **Function:** Menu that lists all the SketchUp commands that can receive keyboard shortcuts.

3. **Add Shortcut:** Add a keyboard shortcut to the item from the menu selected in **2**.

4. **Assigned:** Show the keyboard shortcut(s) used for the menu command(s) selected in **2**.

5. **Reset All:** Delete all the keyboard shortcuts from the record.

6. **Import...:** Import pre-configured keyboard shortcuts.

7. **Export...:** Export current keyboard shortcuts to a file that can be imported at another time.

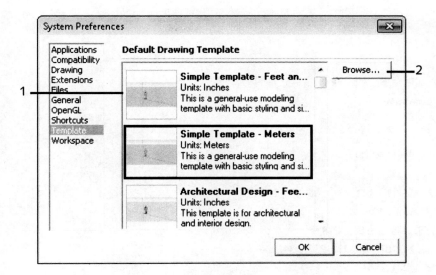

Templates

1. In this list are documents that can be used as templates. The selected document is used as a reference for starting new SketchUp projects.

2. **Browse...**: Click this button to include a SketchUp document in the list of templates.

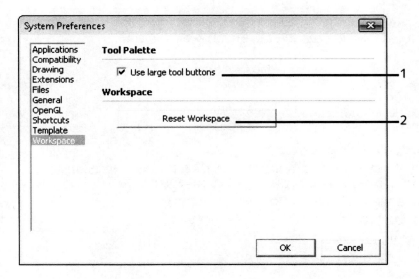

Workspace

1. **Use large tool buttons**: Click to increase the size of the palette buttons.

2. **Reset Workspace**: Click this button so the position of SketchUp tools and menus return to the position that they were at the time the program was installed.

Index

Paperback or e-book?
English, spanish, or portuguese?
Don´t worry, you'll always get the best SketchUp book!

www.thesketchupbook.com   www.librosketchup.com   www.livrosketchup.com.br

CPSIA information can be obtained at www.ICGtesting.com
Printed in the USA
BVOW05s1234150115

383282BV00004B/33/P